PRAISE FOR *BEYOND HIGH PERFORMANCE*

"As one of the world's leading executive coaches, Jason Jaggard is a true master of motivation. Read this book to learn how to make the most of your potential—in business and in life."

Dr. Sandeep Jauhar, speaker, cardiologist, and *New York Times* **bestselling author of** *Heart: A History*

—————————————————————➤

"This book is the ultimate resource for anyone searching to continuously grow in every aspect of their life."

Andrew Ladd, two-time Stanley Cup-winning hockey player

—————————————————————➤

"If you truly believe your leadership has no limits, then I highly recommend this compelling read by Jason Jaggard. He understands the unique strategies and authentic approaches each leader needs to take to achieve their unlimited potential. It's a required playbook for a life of success."

Mayor Justin M. Bibb, Cleveland, Ohio

—————————————————————➤

"*Beyond High Performance* is more than a book full of insights and wisdom—it may be what you've been searching for your entire career. This is a book you will read again and again, generating new insights and new levels of performance every time."

Mark Miller, vice president of High Performance Leadership at Chick-fil-A

"Jason is a friend who has inspired and challenged me but most of all cared for me. He'll do the same for you in his new book. Like our conversations, Jason offers a space to begin thinking in ways you never have. It's not just a great read but a great resource to explore what it is that matters most."

Jeff Henderson, best-selling author of *Know What You're FOR*, CEO of The For Company

---

"A simple truth: only read this book if you want to be inspired to go beyond what you think is possible. The choice is yours!"

Kevin Carroll, speaker, author of *Rules of the Red Rubber Ball*, and once called "The Mayor of Nike" by Phil Knight

---

"Jaggard's *Beyond High Performance* opened my eyes to new possibilities, new approaches, and new ideas in how I live, interact with others, and lead."

Mateo Messina, Grammy Award–winning composer

"Great anecdotes are one thing, but connecting them to real-life application in a lucid and teachable way takes real skill. Jaggard hits a home run here!"

R. A. Dickey, 2012 Cy Young Award-winning Major League Baseball pitcher

---

"This book is like a lifetime membership to a gym, where if you're willing to put in the work, you may just change the world."

Scott Brooks, CEO of Liv Communities

"I like reading books that shift my paradigm. This is a book about leadership and coaching, sure. But it's also about using those skills to explore what matters most. Read it and never see yourself or the world the same way again."

Harris III, storyteller, speaker, author of *The Wonder Switch*, **founder of The Istoria Collective**

"I've struggled with the tension between achieving more and experiencing contentment with the incredible life I already have. The tools in this book have helped me unlock myself in ways I didn't know were possible, in ways that have created both the greater impact and the greater satisfaction that I long for."

Mark Wittig, finance manager at HOH Water Technology, INC

"If you are interested in creating a legacy that will last while you are living, then this book is for you. It completely altered the way I think about my actions and the purpose of them. I live differently now."

Tayt Odom, D1 Training—Fight 6:12 Fitness, LLC

"Jason doesn't care about what his clients *want*; he cares deeply about uncovering the false boundaries we put on our abilities, exposing our true potential to achieve beyond our wildest dreams and ultimately play a part in changing the world. Working with Jason was transformative, enhancing not only my professional performance but deepening the most important personal relationships in my life. Our work together continues to shape my day-to-day business operations and pushes my performance beyond selfish gain. *Beyond High Performance* will push readers to uncover what they truly are capable of achieving."

Tara Hannaford, senior vice president of 21 Holdings LLC

"This book is a love letter to high performers who desire more satisfaction in their lives. It gives them a strategy with principles and tips to transform their lives and the world around them."

Aja Brown, former mayor of Compton, California

"*Beyond High Performance* is for those who want to level up or help others level up their game. A must-read."

Connor McDavid, captain of the NHL's Edmonton Oilers

"Jason and his Novus Global team will give you an insatiable hunger for growth and the courage to choose growth over comfort. If we truly want to keep growing as people, as businesses, and as communities, we have to stop focusing on being the best and start focusing on what we're capable of. This book is the right first step in changing your focus. Going after goals that seem impossible by implementing the frameworks and tools in this book has helped us to launch through seemingly unbreakable ceilings at work and in our personal lives."

Kurt Luginbuhl, president of Interior Services

———————————————————→

"*Beyond High Performance* is clear, compelling, and can change your life. Jaggard takes you on a journey inside yourself, revealing the gifts you never knew where there."

Dan Goods, award-winning artist, creative director, and speaker

———————————————————→

"This book gives insight into the single most important lesson of life—that is, we are all born for growth. If you are ready to live the life of your dreams, I invite you to open the cover."

Chris Ramsey, director of DENSO Corp.

"Jason has a gift for calling us all to a higher standard. He helps us work and live in such an intentional way that reaches our greatest potential."

Caitlin Crosby, founder and CEO, the Giving Keys, and named to Oprah's SuperSoul100 Visionaries and Influencers

---

"Most leaders look for a model or template for how to accomplish a higher level of performance. Jason Jaggard and the Novus Global team go beyond a simplistic framework to provide a completely different way of thinking—a truly new paradigm that can help you rise above what you think you can do and grow into the greatness for which you were created. A must-read for anyone who wants to achieve at their highest level!"

Tom DeVries, president and CEO of the Global Leadership Network

---

"*Beyond High Performance* eloquently summarizes the discoveries I got to make while coaching with Jason and his team. Through my own transformation, I moved from a mindset of scarcity to abundance and discovered the beautiful potential in myself, my team, and my family. The new systems I created allow me to continue the journey to be the best version of myself, and the impact of abundance will change generations to come."

Bill Foy, director of Global Automotive at AWS

"As an agent for Major League Baseball players, I live in a world of high performers. Jason Jaggard and his team at Novus Global have been my secret sauce. In *Beyond High Performance*, they've written a must-read for anyone interested in becoming crystal clear on what it takes to reach the heights of their potential. This book single-handedly steers you down a path of achievement and helps you uncover things that you never considered possible."

Matt Hannaford, MLBPA player agent, president and CEO of ALIGND

───────────────────────────────────➤

"Jaggard is that rare thinker who can take very complex ideas and make them not only understandable but exciting to read and easy to apply."

Trevor Baldwin, president and CEO of Baldwin Risk Partners

Beyond High Performance

What Great Coaches Know About How the Best Get Better

amplifypublishinggroup.com

Beyond High Performance: What Great Coaches Know About How the Best Get Better

For more information, please contact:
Amplify Publishing, an imprint of Amplify Publishing Group
620 Herndon Parkway, Suite 320
Herndon, VA 20170
info@amplifypublishing.com

Library of Congress Control Number: 2023900489

CPSIA Code: PRV0223A

ISBN-13: 978-1-63755-496-8

Printed in the United States

To the clients of Novus Global and the
graduates of the Meta Performance Institute:

We love being fierce advocates for you.

In your success, we find our own.

Never stop going beyond high performance.

BEYOND HIGH PERFORMANCE

WHAT GREAT COACHES KNOW
ABOUT HOW THE BEST GET BETTER

JASON JAGGARD
WITH THE COACHES OF NOVUS GLOBAL AND
THE FACULTY OF THE META PERFORMANCE™ INSTITUTE

an imprint of Amplify Publishing Group

CONTENTS

FOREWORD

Not long after I became president and CEO of Rockefeller Group—a multibillion-dollar real estate developer and investor headquartered in Manhattan—I found myself talking to one of our joint venture partners about my executive coach and my frustration with our lack of progress. I felt that both the company and I should be getting more value out of the investment of time and money. As a first-time CEO, with only a few months in my new role, I had quickly learned that when the discussions and debate were over, all eyes were on me to make the tough calls and the most impactful decisions. I intuitively knew I needed more to succeed at this next level.

My business partner suggested, "You might be interested in talking to this guy who I've worked with, Jason Jaggard."

Soon after that, Jason and I connected. We started talking, and I was intrigued by the questions he asked me and the concept of Meta Performance, so I decided to hire Jason as my new executive coach.

I soon discovered that one of the most helpful—and at times incredibly annoying—things when working with Jason is that he asks so many questions. In every session, he would ask, "What would be most valuable to talk about today? How can we make this the most powerful sixty minutes of your week?"

Part of me wanted to reply, "If I knew that, I wouldn't have hired you!" But after years of working together, I understand this is a critical part of the process. It's classic Jason. He is never going to provide you with the answer. It's always going to be another question. And it's the questions that have been the game changer for our organization and for me.

A few months after Jason and I began working together, our company hired his team at Novus Global to work with our senior executives and business line leaders. In the years since, we have held company-wide video learning sessions led by Novus coaches on Zoom and expanded the coaching to the managing director, VP, director, and associate levels.

With Novus Global's help, we've achieved successes that would have been considered impossible just a few years ago. We've grown our pipeline of deals by over three times since 2019, recorded the most profitable development project in the history of the company in 2020, won numerous design awards for our projects, and been recognized multiple times as one of the top places to work. While 2021 was our most financially successful year in a decade and a half, we fully expect to do better this year. And we're on pace to meet our ten-year goals for financial performance three years early.

Jason and his team have been vital to our success. I'll never forget when we did a two-day group coaching program with our senior leadership team. In one session, I watched the evolution of "impossible to improbable to potential to inevitable" over twenty minutes of conversation. When Jason asked this question, "How could you triple your business in five years?" the discussion evolved from "That's really not possible" and "We can't do that" to "Well, we would need to hire a whole bunch of people" and "We would need to meaningfully grow into new asset classes and new cities." Watching people go from "There's just no way" to "We can do this; we just have to decide to do it" has been integral to unlocking the realm of the possible for us. At the time, the number we wrote down felt intimidating. Now we want to know: "What else are we capable of?"

In *Beyond High Performance*, Jason walks you through what he and Novus Global did for me, my team, and so many other clients. He helps you rethink your perceptions of high performance. Just like he does in coaching, he's not giving you the answers, the how-tos, the this-is-what-you-do-next. Rather, he helps you find the most powerful questions to ask and provides the framework to discover the answers.

If you are even remotely intrigued by the notion that you can do more, that you are capable of more, then you will love this book. Or perhaps you've wondered, *Maybe there's a better way to approach work. Maybe there's a better approach to relationships in my professional and personal life.* And if even the smallest part of you is wondering, *Maybe I could be doing more. Perhaps I am just scratching the surface,* then you have come to the right place. The work that Jason and the Novus Global coaches do, and what Jason has shared in *Beyond High Performance*, will be invaluable in helping you explore these crucial questions. And let me give you a spoiler: *you are capable of so much more than you believe right now.*

Be prepared to look at everything you do in a new way, because once you start asking these questions, like Jason, you won't be able to stop—and the possibilities for you and your team are limitless.

→Daniel J. Moore

SEVEN WORDS THAT CHANGE EVERYTHING

In 1982, Tony Cavallo was sweating in the Georgia heat working underneath a vintage Chevrolet Impala. Suddenly, the car slipped off its jacks onto Tony's chest. Instead of crushing him, Tony felt the three thousand pounds of weight begin to slowly rise off his body. He strained to see who was lifting the car and was shocked to discover not the legs of his coworkers but the familiar stockings of his mother. His aging mom had lifted the car just enough for two neighbors to replace the jacks and pull Tony out from underneath. Once Tony was out of danger, he and his neighbors looked at his mom in disbelief. No one was more surprised than her. She whispered to herself, "I didn't know I could do that."[1]

The phenomenon of bursts of enhanced ability has a name in medical circles: *hysterical strength*.[2] Apparently, stored up in each person, under the right conditions, are abilities people don't realize they have. There have been documented cases of extraordinary strength peppered throughout history: a family saved from a burning building. Babies rescued from ice-filled rivers. And yes, even cars lifted off the chests of men by their mothers. Over and over, with singed hair or soaking clothes or trembling knees, people have whispered those seven words: "I didn't know I could do that."

While these stories are usually about *physical* feats of strength, there are other examples of uncommon abilities that don't involve, you know, lifting things. In the worlds of business, activism, sports, entertainment, and even relationships, there are moments of what could be called hysterical strength. As the US Olympic Hockey Team beat the Soviets in the 1980 Winter Games, sportscaster Al Michaels screamed, "Do you believe in miracles?!" (Read: "I didn't know they could do that!") Or after Walt Disney opened his first theme park bearing his name he said, "It's kind of fun to do the impossible." Or in 1994, after leading South Africa to end apartheid, Nelson Mandela said, "It always seems impossible until it's done." To paraphrase Walt and Nelson: we didn't know we could do that . . . until we did.

On a smaller scale, that's the experience many of us have when we lead our teams in a new way or when we create something we've never created before. It's how we feel when we accomplish something extraordinary together with people we love. It can be a bizarre and disorienting experience finding ourselves doing something we didn't know we could do. Sometimes it's uncomfortable. But most of the time the experience is wonderful. Intoxicating. And I believe this is one of the greatest thrills of being alive. When we go beyond what we think we're capable of, and while we're doing *that thing*, we smile and think, *I didn't know I could do that.*

I want you to have that experience as often as possible.

This book is about you doing what you don't realize you can do.

And for those of us who like to dream a little bigger, this book is about what our companies and communities can do that they don't realize they can do.

May we all experience hysterical strength in the things that matter most.

Let's begin.

→ "It can be a bizarre and disorienting experience finding ourselves doing something we didn't know we can do. Sometimes it's uncomfortable. But most of the time the experience is wonderful."

INTRODUCTION
THE INNER WORLD OF HIGH PERFORMERS

I love high performers. And if you're reading this, you're probably one of them. Tell me if any of this sounds familiar:[1] the dirty little secret of high performers is that they *simultaneously*

a) highly believe in themselves

b) know they're capable of more

c) are a little nervous of what "more" might entail.

High performers are a wonderful cocktail of seemingly conflicting beliefs. According to our research with our clients all over the world, 89 percent of those surveyed reported sometimes feeling like imposters—fake it *even after* you make it—and 71 percent reported occasionally feeling like anyone could do their job. In other words, while others might be impressed with them, they are not that impressed with themselves. At the same time, high performers take a degree of pride in being *very* good at their work. They get frustrated when others don't show up like they do. And yet they tend to fluctuate between enjoying being *really* good at what they do and worrying they aren't good enough.

How can they truly know if they're coasting or doing their best? The question is harder to answer than it may seem. The Stoic philosopher Seneca once said, "No one can ever know what you are capable of, not even you."[2] And this is the problem of potential: How do we *really* know what it is we're capable of? High performers wrestle with questions like these:

What is beneath me (and not worth my time)?

What is out of my reach (and not worth the risk)?

You may also read this and think, *I know I could do more and that I am capable of more, but what?*

And at what cost?

If you ever find yourself asking these questions, then this book is for you.

BEHIND THE SCENES WITH THE BEST

Over the last twenty years, I've had an up-close-and-personal look at high performers. As a coach and founder of Novus Global[3]—our international executive coaching firm—and cofounder of the Meta Performance Institute[4]—a nontraditional incubator for coaches, leaders, and managers—our teams have worked with executives of Fortune 100 companies, elected officials, professional athletes, world-renowned artists and movie stars, and multimillionaires. At the firm, our clients go beyond their own levels of high performance. At the institute, we have the privilege of helping some of the best leaders in the world learn how to coach like we do. We have been fortunate enough to learn what helps the best get better from *actually being in the trenches with them*, behind the scenes, coaching them to greater performance for both them and their teams. And while I've been journeying with high performers for a long time, my admiration for them started back when I was a kid.

And I bet yours did too.

One thing you and I probably have in common is that we both had people we looked up to when we were younger. For me, I looked up to musicians. Usually, dead ones. The first album I ever bought was *Bennie Goodman Live at Carnegie Hall* (recorded in 1938). I played the trumpet at the time—my poor parents—and I remember being blown away (pun intended) by Bennie's Big Band just annihilating "Sing with a Swing." I listened to that song over and over and over again because, as a trumpet player, Benny's band was the best. Or maybe it was athletes. A lot of us reading this probably remember watching the Olympics on a couch somewhere, transfixed by the drama of the best athletes sacrificing years of their lives for one shot to do something extraordinary. And being raised in the nineties meant *sports* was spelled with two words: *Michael Jordan*. Even kids who were horrible at basketball—that would be me; after all, I was a "musician"—would stick out our tongues and lunge from the free-throw line with our arms outstretched, flying through the air, if only in our imaginations. Michael Jordan was the GOAT. And I, like other kids around the world, was drawn to that. Or take film and television: I remember Marla Brassfield taking a bunch of us kids to see *The Little Mermaid* in 1988. I'll never forget walking out of that grimy theater, with my tennis shoes sticking to the dried-soda floor, understanding that I had just seen a work of art. I told myself, *I want to be around people who tell stories like* that *someday.*

Looking back, I can now see how this admiration for the best eventually led to me founding the firm and then years later co-founding the institute with one of our top coaches (and also my biological sister), Amanda. My early love of music and musicians found its fulfillment in a coaching firm, where we've had coaches who sang with Prince and clients who have won Grammys. An admiration for athletes turned into a firm where we have clients who are some of the highest-paid athletes in the history of the world and where some of our graduates of the institute are former professional athletes themselves. And years after *The Little Mermaid* our coaches not only have been on the Disney Studio lot working with their leaders but we've had the privilege of serving A-list celebrities and some of the most creative filmmakers in Hollywood. Among the coaches in our firm and the faculty of the institute, there are over one hundred years of combined coaching and leadership wisdom working with some of the highest performers in the world, and the book you're holding contains some of our best understanding from working with these extraordinary people and helping them step into their next level of greatness.

IS GREATNESS FOR EVERYONE?

Some reading this might be thinking, *Hooray for you and your clients, but that's not for everyone. Only a few people are destined to be great.* Let me humbly suggest: All people are designed for greatness. You. Me. That jerk at work you don't like. Everyone. Pablo Picasso once said, "Every child is an artist. The problem is how to remain an artist once we grow up." Is it possible that the same could be true about greatness? We're all born designed to admire those who can lift what we can't—like when our dads picked us up, and we thought he was the strongest man on earth—or admire people who are smarter than us, like when our moms knew why the sky was blue. As we grew older, we all looked to rock stars, Pulitzer Prize winners, role models we had at school, business moguls, activists, artists, elected officials, or titans of history. There's something about greatness that has a gravitational pull. There is beauty in simply seeing someone do something with excellence. But I want to strongly suggest that the real beauty isn't simply in beholding it but in becoming it. There is power not only in perceiving greatness but in pursuing it. Is it possible that our desire to perceive greatness is the evidence that we were meant to pursue it?

Believe it or not, I was taught this since I was a child at (brace yourself) church of all places. I actually grew up in a fantastic, albeit imperfect, spiritual community, where my mentors and youth leaders constantly encouraged me to believe that the purpose of life was to pursue

→ "Is it possible that our desire to perceive greatness is the evidence that we were meant to pursue it?"

greatness. I had some of the best youth leaders a young person could ask for. One of them, Darren Wade, wrote me a note when I was young that I have kept all these years. He told me, "Never be satisfied." He pounded that message into me in every speech he gave. It was an encouragement that said, "There's always more, and while there is nothing wrong with being content, do not let contentment drift into complacency and rob you of the life you are meant to live."

And this is the tension we high performers find ourselves in: the never-ending tug-of-war between contentment and complacency. High performers have a lot to be content about, and yet they also have this itch that there's more. This naturally causes a sense of internal struggle. Oftentimes high performers will accidentally choose complacency instead of contentment as a salve against that pathological need for more. They have this "love-hate" relationship with the idea of "more." Some have burned out on pursuing more at any cost. Others have gotten everything they've ever wanted, and they still feel unfulfilled. Still others choose to get off the work treadmill completely. They radically shift their priorities and simplify their lives by going to some other country as a spiritual tourist for a year and coming back zenned out, wearing loose-fitting clothes and detached from the world they used to be obsessed with. It seems as though the choice is to either sacrifice yourself on the altar of "more" or to run away from the "more monster" altogether.

I want to suggest a third way: You don't have to want less. And you don't have to destroy yourself in the pursuit of more. And that's the question I really want you to sit with: *What if it were possible for you to accomplish more without it ruining your life?* Or more importantly: What if it were possible for you to accomplish more in a way that *enhances* your life? Most of us believe that in order to grow or take our lives to the next level we have to destroy everything in the process. But for us at the firm and the institute, we believe there's a way to pursue more from a healthy and sober place and in a way that is a gift to you, the people you work with, and those you love.

This book will show you how.

→ "You don't have to want less. And you don't have to destroy yourself in the pursuit of more."

THIS BOOK IS NOT ABOUT (ONLY) YOU

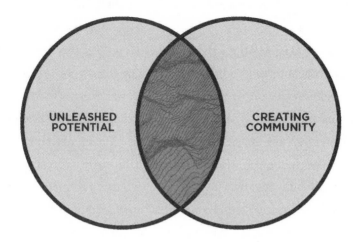

UNLEASHED POTENTIAL

CREATING COMMUNITY

The pages ahead of you reflect two obsessions me and my colleagues at the firm and the institute have: an obsession with unleashing the potential in others and an obsession with community. This book is the intersection of those two things, which might sound strange coming from a coach. You may not have noticed, but most coaches you probably know are solopreneurs. Many find their way into the coaching world because they don't want to work on teams anymore. If you look around at the Great Resignation of 2021, more than ever people were "opting out" and going out on their own. In many ways, this is exciting, but it can also be problematic: here you have a bunch of people leaving teams, many of whom didn't like being on teams, who are now coaching people who are on teams. Hiring a coach who doesn't like being on a team is like hiring a dentist who doesn't like teeth.

Our companies are different. When we started the firm, we were committed to a team approach to coaching. We truly believe we are better together. We created the firm because we want to create a community of coaches who all have this fierce conviction that the best way to explore what you're capable of is in the context of the community. And when we started the institute, it's because we wanted to give others the tools to fall in love with the sacred arts of coaching and leading and managing that we love so much. We believed that if we put out the message that we're looking for and aspiring toward greatness the right people would come. This reminds me of something said by Nick Fury, played by the inimitable Samuel L. Jackson, in the 2012 movie *The Avengers*, which brought together Captain America, the Hulk, Iron Man, Thor, Black Widow, and Hawkeye—all stars, all deserving of their own franchises, all high performers. Walking around a table filled with Marvel's biggest names, Fury makes the case for bringing them all together: "There was an idea . . . the idea was to bring together a group of remarkable people, to see if they could become something more." Even though that's a quote from a comic-book movie full of people whose primary superpower is fitting their sculpted figures into spandex outfits, it still gets me every time. And if it gets you too, even just a little bit, then I think the ideas and suggested habits in the following pages might just change your life.

HOW TO USE THIS BOOK

I want you to think of this book as proverbial gym equipment you will "work out with" to reach incredible new levels of impact in your life. And like all workouts, it's not a one-and-done event. Our hope is that the ideas in this book will become some of your favorite "weights" to wrestle with and bench-press into the muscle of your life. And while this was written for any person who wants to explore going beyond high performance, there's a few other specific groups of people we want to highlight who might be reading. If you're an aspiring coach, or someone who uses coaching principles in their life and leadership, this book is an essential piece of gym equipment for the people you serve. For those of you who have benefited from our coaching over the years and wish your teams could have a basic understanding of what it is you are wanting them to achieve, this book is for you to pass along to them. If you are one of our graduates from the institute, we wrote this as a resource for you as well. But mostly we wrote this for anyone who senses they have an extra gear inside them that they're wanting to shift into in order to make a greater contribution to their world. These values and methods have helped the companies we've worked with make billions of dollars and give out millions of dollars of bonuses and philanthropy. It's helped employees get more done in less time, increased employee satisfaction, reduced costs, fund vacation and college budgets, and so much more. Since I know not every one of you has a coach or will go through our institute, this book can be like a "coach on your shoulder" and will be the next best thing for you, your team, and your organization.

Next, when you're reading along, you don't have to agree with what you read. In fact, disagreement is important. Do your own thinking. But if you disagree, it will be important that you notice and then get curious about why—why you resonate with some things and not with others. There's probably going to be some things in here that might even offend you. I promise that's not on purpose. But I also promise if you get offended, there is value in exploring the offense. All offense is designed to protect something. I recommend you get curious about where the offense is coming from and ask yourself: Does the belief your offense is protecting serve you or hurt you?

In this way, we believe coaching is a form of meditation. Granted, it is a high-octane, relational form of meditation, during which you are paying attention to yourself in a new way with a new lens, with a new listening, so that you can create things that currently are invisible to you and/or might seem to be impossible for you. I want you to read this as a form of meditation in a way that makes you pay attention to yourself. Listen to the invitation from the pages ahead to step into something new and extraordinary and pay attention to what happens or how you react, feel, or create while you do it. The book you hold isn't really the content. As we say at the firm and institute: *you are the content.*

Finally, seek more than insights. Most people receive accidental value from books. Most of us read because we're interested in a subject, and then if we're lucky we get an ah-ha moment or an insight. And then if you're really lucky that insight translates into some kind of interesting anecdote at a cocktail party or an interesting quote to pass around the office or mention in a meeting, and that's about it. In other words, the book didn't really change your life; it just changed what you talked about for a couple of weeks. Lori Gottlieb, psychologist and author of *Maybe You Should Talk to Someone: A Therapist, Her Therapist, and Our Lives Revealed,* writes, "Insight is

→ "The book you hold isn't really the content. As we say at the firm and institute: *you are the content.*"

the booby prize of therapy."[5] That's one of my favorite maxims of the trade. What she means is you can have insights galore, but if you don't apply anything when you're out in the world, the insight and the therapy is nearly worthless. Don't let the insights get in the way of making progress. While we hope every chapter is packed with paradigm-shifting, consciousness-expanding insights, we also hope those insights are not the end of your journey. They are just the beginning.

IT WORKS (IF YOU WORK IT)

The ideas in this book have changed my life and have changed the lives of people all over the world who long to go beyond high performance. I'll never forget being asked to fly to New York to speak at one of our client's corporate events. They'd had their best year ever—an increased sales pipeline of several hundred million dollars—and had attributed a large part of their success to the work that our coaches had done with their executive leadership and management teams. I was at the after-party of the event, in a Midtown skyscraper with huge windows of the greatest city on earth, with a live band and lots of champagne for the celebration.

"Jason!" I heard someone yell over the music. I turned to see a huge, burly leader in New York business walk up to me, wrap his arms around me, and lift me off the ground. These kinds of gruff types aren't prone to signs of affection, and I was caught off guard.

"I want to thank your team for what they've done for me," he said. "Not only have I had my best year ever in business, but I've been using the tools I learned through coaching with my sixteen-year-old daughter, and it's really helped our relationship." Then he teared up—these guys never tear up—and he said, "In the past, her mom was the one she really connected to, but going through adolescence has put a strain on their relationship, and I've been able to step up and connect with her . . ." He paused, and said, "I didn't know I could do that." And he reached his huge hand out to shake mine and said, "Thank you."

This is what I want for you. If a guy at the top of his game can go even further professionally, if a rough-and-tough businessman can reinvent his relationship with his teenage daughter, then imagine what you can do. If I've done my job right, by the time you're finished reading this book, you, too, will feel the same exuberance, energy, and gratitude and will have transcended the ordinary to the incredible, and you will have done it with others.

In part 1 of this book, I will teach you the three ways most people perceive work, and the fourth way that will transform how you'll see work for the rest of your life (chapter 1). We'll explore together the most common ways high performers hold themselves back and what to do about it (chapter 2). We'll talk about one of the most important tools for high performers that they almost always underutilize (chapter 3). Some of the chapters you can apply immediately (like chapter 4 on culture), but the more powerful chapters will be ones that gradually reshape how you see yourself, how you see others, and how you see the world around you. And perhaps most importantly, in part 2, you will learn the hallmark principles of the GO LIVE mindset we practice with our clients at the firm and with our coaches-in-training at the institute. GO LIVE is an acronym inviting you to explore

→ how to increase your obsession for *growth* without burning out;

→ how to leverage *ownership* like a searchlight, looking for strength and agency you didn't know you had;

→ how to use *love* as your secret weapon when it comes to accomplishing intimidating goals;

→ how the word *integrity* isn't what you think it is, and how you can use it as one of the fastest ways to get more done in less time;

→ how to use *vision* to reshape your present—and even your past—to create a better future; and

→ how to cultivate more *energy* in your life that spreads to others in powerful ways.

Our hope for you is that you will discover what eludes even those at the rarified top, all so that you can go beyond high performance.

But our first stop is a journey into your mind and how to redesign it to create what you and your teams can now only dream of.

PART 1
THE META-
PERFORMING MIND

When I was a kid, my parents forced me to write thank-you notes to relatives for gifts they gave me. I hated it. Not because I hated writing notes, although I suppose I hated that too, but because the "gifts" I was being asked to be grateful for usually sucked (sorry, distant relatives). I wasn't grateful for them. Writing a note wasn't going to magically make me grateful. In fact, writing a thank-you note made me less grateful because now there were *two* things in my life I never asked for: a horrible gift *and* the task of writing a note. Of course, my parents may have felt good because they got one kind of result—that is, a thank-you note sent to said relative to pay the "thankful tax" expected when gifts were given, no matter how bad the gifts were. But they didn't get the *deeper* kind of result they really wanted: helping me actually learn to be grateful. In fact, forcing a little rug rat like me to write "thank you" for the cheap, oversized sunglasses that I'd never wear not only didn't teach me to be grateful; it taught me how to fake gratitude to make others happy. This is because gratitude doesn't flow from writing a note. It flows from seeing life as a gift, or developing what we might call a "gratitude mindset." If you can help a child cultivate a grateful mind, then spontaneous actions of gratitude will begin to emerge that you, as a parent, would never anticipate.

The goal isn't to change one behavior; the goal is to change your mind. You can learn tips, habits, and tricks about something, but they usually won't produce the lasting results you want, because you haven't yet changed your mind. This doesn't mean there aren't things you can do to redesign your mind. There are. And that's what part 1 of this book is about. Just like creating a mind of gratitude, we're inviting you into the creation of a certain kind of mind that naturally goes beyond high performance. In this section, we want to teach you a certain way of seeing the world. We want to teach you a certain way of seeing yourself. We want to introduce you to a certain kind of mind. The following principles are designed to provide scaffolding, an agile structure, to help retrain your mind to perceive existence differently, out of which spontaneous new behaviors will begin to emerge. This is what we do in coaching with all our clients. We don't tell them what to do. We're building a system in which they can redesign their minds. And once they have a mind designed to go beyond high performance, they start performing in ways that surprise even themselves.

→ "The goal isn't to change one behavior; the goal is to change your mind."

CHAPTER 1

THE PRISONER, THE MERCENARY, AND THE MISSIONARY

It's just a job: grass grows, birds fly, waves pound the sand. I beat people up.

→ **MUHAMMAD ALI**

New Year's Eve—One Hundred Million Dollars—Private Islands—Tinfoil Handcuffs—It's Just Business—The Invisible Athlete—Getting Reps—What Comes after Malcolm Gladwell

WHAT IS WORK FOR: A TALE
OF TWO CAREERS

New Year's Eve, 2015. Hollywood, California. I'm at a swanky bar. My friends are in Gatsby suits and go-go dresses, and the party is swinging. Over the course of the night, I end up standing next to a decently accomplished LA artist. We start talking about work. "What's your goal with your work?" I asked him.

"Easy!" he shouted over the crowd counting down to 2016. "I want to work hard, cash out, and live on a beach somewhere for the rest of my life!"

Fast-forward a year later. Santa Monica, California. I'm on a restaurant balcony overlooking the Pacific Ocean as the sun sets. I'm having a conversation with a woman who had started several successful accessory companies, selling her first company for over $100 million. She never has to work again. She has just accomplished what our earlier LA artist friend could only dream of. So I ask her, "What was that like, exiting your first company and being free from work forever?"

"I told myself I would take two years off before jumping into my next venture," she replies.

I smile and ask, "How many 'years' did you end up taking off?"

She laughs. "About two months."

She and I look knowingly at each other, and she adds, "But they were a good two months."

Why did she jump back into work so quickly? Why didn't she buy an island and live the rest of her life in luxury and ease? If you asked her, she'd tell you: It's not because she's a workaholic. Certainly it's not because she needs the money. It's that she understands human beings are, in part, *designed* for work. I can't tell you how many people are like the LA artist who thinks the goal of life is to not work. Or maybe, put another way, most people think the purpose of work is to eventually stop working. We work now so that someday we won't have to. We work now so we can retire later. Maybe you're reading this, and you think it is too. But we want to suggest that work is for something else.

LIFE AFTER MALCOM GLADWELL

Millions of people have been introduced to Dr. Anders Ericcson's concept of ten thousand hours,[1] made famous by Malcom Gladwell in his bestselling book *Outliers: The Story of Success*. Gladwell argues that you, anyone, could become a master in any given field if you were able to dedicate ten thousand hours of practice toward it. He cites a wide variety of examples, from the Beatles to Bill Gates, all of whom practiced for ten thousand hours before "making it." Then, Michael Miller, in an article for Six Seconds, explains the caveat to the ten-thousand-hour rule, mainly arguing that all practice isn't equal by explaining Dr. Ericcson's concept of "deliberate practice." Miller writes, "The best way to get better at something is through something known as deliberate practice, which means practicing in order to get better: doing activities recommended by experts to develop specific abilities, identifying weaknesses, and working to correct them, and intentionally pushing yourself out of your comfort zone."[2] Michael Sullivan quotes the researcher Ericsson, who said, "Not every type of practice leads to improved ability. You don't get benefits from mechanical repetition, but by adjusting your execution over and over to get closer to your goal."[3]

What Gladwell, Ericsson, and Miller all agree on is that the point of the ten-thousand-hour rule is to get good at something. Really good. And that's how most high performers relate to work. Get good at something, get well paid at something. Bull's-eye. Nailed it. And while we agree that getting really good at something is a worthy use of ten thousand hours, we also think they're missing a broader point for high performers, which is this: *What happens after ten thousand hours?* The ten-thousand-hour rule is fantastic if the goal of work is to get really good at something. But what happens after you're already good? The reality is, most of us will dedicate ten thousand hours to *something.* That's the first ten years of your career. Or if you start developing your skills in your teens, like many do, then you've got your ten thousand hours down in your twenties. Most of us reading this already have our ten thousand hours or are close to it. Some of us have deliberately practiced, some of us haven't, but if you're reading this you've probably already spent ten thousand hours doing *something.*

Now what?

That's the deeper question the Beatles had to answer. That's the deeper question Bill Gates and every professional athlete has to answer. It's the question every high performer has to answer. It's probably the question you have to answer: What do you do after you're already great at something? After you write "Hard Day's Night." *After* you invent Microsoft Office? What do you do *after* your ten thousand hours? To answer that, we have to look at what comes *after* the ten-thousand-hour rule.

HOW MANY HOURS WILL YOU WORK?

Imagine you could take all the activities of your life and clump them together into categories of time. For example, think about how many hours you'll spend with your loved ones. Think about how much time you'll spend sleeping. Think about how much time you'll spend on vacation or how much time you'll spend raising kids or staring at a screen or going to the bathroom.

Now I want you to think about how much time you'll spend *at work*. I'm going to tell you something that might be a little depressing: according to the best estimates, you will spend more time at work than nearly any other activity in your life. You will spend some time asleep, in school, socializing, building families, working out at the gym, or arguing with a lover, but by and large, the majority of your waking hours will be spent working. In fact, according to the research of Andrew Naber, an industrial and organizational psychologist and an associate behavioral scientist at RAND Corporation, we humans now spend on average about a third of life at a job. That averages out to be about one hundred thousand hours doing something you call "work."

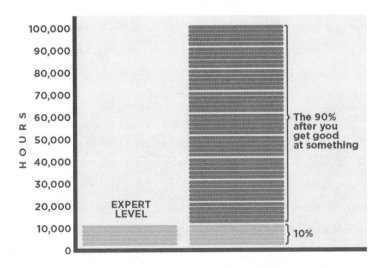

One hundred thousand hours.

This means how you look at work is one of the most important things that will ever shape your life. Most people talk about how they relate to money or how they relate to relationships, but very few people talk about how they relate to work. Yet how you relate to work is one of the most important relationships you'll ever have.

In our world at the firm and the institute, we love the ten-thousand-hour rule, but we're more interested in the one-hundred-thousand-hour rule (notice we haven't told you what it is yet—don't worry; keep reading). Whether you like it or not, you're going to be spending one hundred thousand hours of your life at work. Which begs the question: What's the best way to spend one hundred thousand hours? I want you to stop for a moment and think about this: How do you want to use them?

This is where your relationship to work comes in. Most people, when they think of relationships and work, think about their relationships *at* work. And a lot of people complain about their relationships *at* work. Bosses who don't get it. Colleagues who don't get it. Employees who don't get it. Clients who don't get it. In many ways, work *is* relationships. Studies have shown that the single greatest contributing factor

→ **"You need to evaluate not your relationships *at* work but your relationship *to* work."**

to people's satisfaction at work are the relationships. One study revealed that 49 percent of people leave their jobs not because of the job itself but because of the relational environment *at* work.[4]

And as important as relationships *at* work are, there's a

relationship that's even more important. You see, to begin exploring going beyond high performance, you need to evaluate not your relationships *at* work but your relationship *to* work. Your relationships at work are about, "Who am I working with?" (we'll touch on this in chapter 3). But your relationship *with* work asks an even bigger question: "What is work *for*?"

The reality is, all of us have a relationship with work, but we're not always aware of it. And just like how not paying attention to our relationships outside work can ruin those relationships, the same thing can happen to our relationship *to* work if we're not careful. We've noticed there are three primary ways people tend to relate to work. They are: the prisoner, the mercenary, and the missionary.

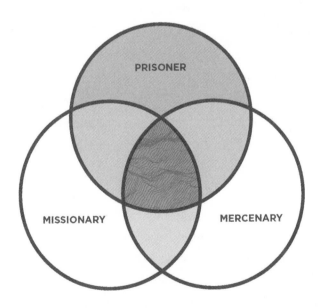

As you read the descriptions below, think about which one resonates with you most. We've found that most high performers drift in and out of each of these three from time to time, but they

tend to have a favorite—a home base—they keep coming back to.
First off, we'll start with the prisoner.

THE PRISONER

The prisoner is the person who does work they don't want to do, because they have to. Simply put, it feels like they don't have a choice. This isn't necessarily because they don't have money, although sometimes this is the case. But I can't tell you how many millionaires, when asked, "Do you love your work?" will say an emphatic no. It's soul crushing. They do it because they have to. They have to keep up with their peers. They have bills to pay. Families to provide for. They don't know what they'd do if they weren't doing their current job. They often feel trapped. We even have a prisoner metaphor for this: "golden handcuffs." But the golden handcuffs don't even have to be all that golden. So long as we feel stuck, the handcuffs could be made out of tinfoil, and we won't break free. Someone with the prisoner mindset doesn't wake up in the morning feeling great about their work. It's something they have to bear and get over with or even dread. They don't necessarily care about being good at their job, insofar as it gets the job done. They don't even have to be great at their job to still make money at it. It can be hard to focus on self-improvement because they are too focused on keeping their head above water, which in their case is the ability to eat and live. In sum, the prisoner works because they're forced to.

THE MERCENARY

The mercenary also works for the money, but unlike the prisoner they love what they do. It's fun. And as soon as it stops being fun, they move elsewhere. They don't care about who they're doing it for.

Just like high-paid prisoners, I know a lot of high-paid executives who love the money and the work more than who they're working with or for. If the sworn enemy of whoever hired them offers them a higher salary to do the same to their current employer, they have no problem switching teams. "It's not personal; it's business." This is a mercenary's mantra. Mercenaries don't necessarily have to be cutthroat either. They don't have a lot of skin in the game. Mercenaries are like babysitters. You can hire someone who loves kids to watch your kids for you. They may love their jobs, and they love the money, but when you come home at night, they're not sticking around. The kids belong to you, not them. They've got a life to live. They clock in, do a great job—often mercenaries are high performers—and clock out. "Work hard, play harder" is another mercenary mantra. They work hard so they can play hard. In other words, the mercenary works to live.

THE MISSIONARY

Missionaries aren't really motivated by money. It's all about the cause for them. These people are usually teachers or run nonprofits or some altruistic organization, but not always. Missionaries also have a way of turning anything into a cause. There are scores of Silicon Valley tech start-ups that truly believe their app or invention is going to change or save the world. Ultimately, they do it because they feel compelled to. Sometimes they are underpaid and underappreciated, but they are fulfilled because they get to be a part of something bigger than themselves. Unlike the mercenary, it's all personal for them; it's never just business. And they don't see what they do as work, but rather as a cause or a purpose. They have the opposite mentality of the mercenary. They often are self-sacrificial and deplete themselves at the expense of the cause. They aren't so much as worried about their survival but their impact. They occasionally put themselves last. Sometimes they don't invest in themselves or they neglect themselves, because they're not concerned with getting personally better. Their only focus is others or their mission, and without it, they feel adrift, almost as if they have lost all purpose or meaning. In other words, for the missionary, work is life.

Doing things you feel like you're forced to do (prisoner), doing things you feel like you want to do (mercenary), and doing things you believe you're called to do (missionary) are all a part of work, and all of us experience all three from time to time, at work and everywhere else. Sometimes I feel trapped like a prisoner—usually during meetings with spreadsheets about budgets and details. Sometimes I love my job and love the money that comes with it—when we get opportunities to work with amazing leaders and business is booming—when our teams are swashbuckling merce-naries for hire coaching powerfully and enjoying the spoils. And many times I'm motivated by the cause of our companies. It's not just a job for me. In many ways, and on many days, it feels like something deeper, like a calling—and as a leader, I try to stay as connected to this as possible. So these mindsets all float around inside me on any given day. They probably float around inside you too. And at any moment we get to choose which one we want to be coming from.

And while most people live in one of these three categories—either doing something they hate to pay the bills, doing something they love to pay the bills, or doing something they love whether it pays the bills or not—at the firm and the institute, we'd like to suggest another way of relating to work. For in each of the previous metaphors, the endgame is either money, self, or a cause. But for this final way, the endgame is something else entirely. And for this kind of relationship, we've chosen to represent it with a fourth metaphor: the athlete.

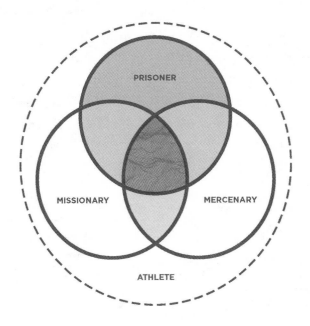

THE ATHLETE

I want you to imagine a world-class athlete at work in your mind. What are they doing? Maybe they're scoring the winning goal in the championship game. Maybe they're holding a trophy in front of thousands. They're probably on a field or court, and there's probably a crowd. But here's the thing: most of the actual "work" of an athlete no one ever sees. Most of an athlete's life isn't spent in front of roaring fans or scoring goals or holding trophies. Most of their work is done in private, without fans, without trophies.

Their work isn't what we think it is.

We have coaches in our firm who have competed at the highest level of sport, and we have clients who are some of the best athletes in the world. They are known for what they've done on the field. Yet if you were to look at the amount of time they spend working with the cameras off compared to the amount of time they spend with cameras on, it's not even close. Another way of putting this is that the primary work of an athlete is invisible. They get up early and hit the ice or the court or the pool or the track or the gym. They strain and sweat and strive and work. To the athlete, practice isn't something you do *before* you go to work. To the athlete, practice *is* the work.

And work is practice.

PRISONER	MERCENARY	MISSIONARY	ATHLETE
I work because I'm forced to.	I work because I want to.	I work because I'm called to.	I work in order to grow.
Work is punishment.	Work to live.	Work is life.	Growth is life.
Work hard, play never.	Work hard, play hard.	Work is play.	Work is practice and practice is play.

An athlete shows up to constantly grow. Athletes engage in exercises during which they push themselves outside their comfort zones, use the feedback of their coaches and team members to get better, and spend their time practicing to be great. Athletes know they can't do it alone. They know a team is depending on them, or their greatness is dependent on their team. While many athletes get well paid, they're putting in the work mostly because they want to constantly be better than they were yesterday. The athlete's work is about constantly getting better. For athletes, work is where they practice growing. Moreover, for athletes, the work is about what it's doing to them as much as what it's doing for them.

WHAT ARE YOU PRACTICING? (OR LIFE AS REPS)

We treat our clients like they are athletes. We know they all have one hundred thousand hours they will be spending at work, and we want them to start thinking of using that time as practice—deliberate practice—for growth.

That's the one-hundred-thousand-hour rule: treating work as an opportunity to get great at growth.

Everyone is practicing something at work all the time. So let me ask you: what are you practicing? For example, every time I show up to a meeting, I'm practicing how to participate in meetings. If I show up give only half my best, I'm practicing becoming the kind of person who doesn't bring my best. I'm training myself how to be, and I'm training others how to perceive me. But every time I'm coaching a client and I bring my best, I am practicing becoming the kind of coach who brings their best. Work is the place where you can spend one hundred thousand hours practicing becoming a certain kind of person. The one-hundred-thousand-hour rule is about being intentional about what kind of person you want to become and then leveraging

→ "That's the one-hundred-thousand-hour rule: treating work as an opportunity to get great at growth."

your hours spent at work—no matter what the job is—to become that kind of person. We believe when everything becomes practice, everyone can maximize their opportunity to grow.

That's the question the one-hundred-thousand-hour rule invites you to ask: What if work was a playground, lab, or gymnasium in which to play, learn, and get your reps in becoming who you long to be? So many people today see work as this life-sucking force. If they're looking at life as an hourglass, every minute they spend at work represents their time running out. It feels depleting. At the end of every day, you're tapped out, and you're counting down the days until vacation or retirement. But what if we could flip that hourglass? What if after one hundred thousand hours you had more skills, more talents, more joy, more success, more friends, more time? What if working wasn't a life-draining but a life-sustaining, life-giving force?

There's something romantic about that. It's not about being forced to work. It's not about doing it just for the paycheck. It's not about work consuming our lives. It's about looking at work as a means of creative output, of adding value. Work is a gift. It's not drudgery. It's not just a means to an end, and not just a place to make money.

We want you to start thinking about work as an athlete.

The one-hundred-thousand-hour rule: You have one hundred thousand hours of work—do what you can to make them count.

 Want to go deeper on this topic? We've developed free resources for you and your team for each chapter, including discussion questions, recorded interviews with our coaches, and more. To access, scan the QR code or go to www.novus.global/book/chapter1.

CHAPTER 2

WHAT COMES AFTER HIGH PERFORMANCE?

To remain relevant in the twenty-first century you will have to reinvent yourself, not just once but repeatedly.

→ YUVAL NOAH HARARI

The Arrested Affect—Infinite Pyramids—Fortune 10 Companies—The High-Performer Problem—That's So Meta—Solutions for Divas—Chik Chik-a-Boom, Chik Chik-a-Boom, Chik Chik-a-Boom

THE POWER OF QUESTIONS

A few years ago, I was brought in to give a talk on the power of questions at the premier conference for storytellers in the world run by my friend Harris III. Yes, that's his actual name; before he turned twenty-one, he made his first million as a magician, and the name stuck. Harris's flagship conference curates one thousand of the top artists, creatives, and entertainers, ranging from Hollywood legends to artists at Nike and *National Geographic* to up-and-coming digital innovators who most people won't hear about for another several years. During my presentation, I told the crowded room about the "arrested effect," which describes how whenever you're asked a question you feel the neurological need to focus on it. You see, questions literally "arrest" our attention, like a kind of police officer for your mind. If I asked you what your name is, you have to fight your impulse—a phenomenon called "instinctive elaboration"—*not* to answer.[1] More than that, questions shape your behavior: In one study, forty thousand people were asked if they plan to buy a car in the next six months. The researchers discovered that asking them that simple question increased their purchase rate by over 34 percent.[2] This is called the "mere measurement effect." If I ask you who you would vote for in an election, you don't just want to tell me who; studies show that you are now *twice as likely* to actually vote—simply because I asked the question.[3] I can increase the probability of you doing something just by asking you about it. This is the power of questions.

Questions arrest us. They compel us. They influence us. In fact, the trajectory of your life is a direct result of the questions you're asking and not asking. So if I can instill any habit in you from reading this book, it would be this: get in the habit of upgrading the questions you're asking.

Especially when it comes to performance.

QUESTIONS THAT DRIVE PERFORMANCE

Since questions shape everything, they also shape your performance. So if you want to increase your performance at something—anything—upgrade the questions you're asking about it.

Because most people don't realize this, I believe most organizations, coaches, and people miss the most important ingredient to increasing performance. This is because they have an incomplete construct by which they are organizing their teams. Current management models typically diagnose employees or teams into three general categories: low performance, performance, and high performance. This can be illustrated by the pyramid below:

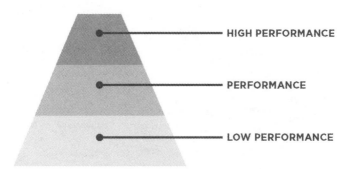

People performing at the three different levels tend to consistently ask themselves different types of questions:

1) People with a low-performance mindset ask the question, "What's the least amount of work I can do and not get fired?" We don't usually say this out loud, but it guides our behavior. Most of the time we don't even see the needs of people around us or the

needs of the organization, because when we have a low-performance mindset, we're too busy thinking about how we can do less, or as little as possible.

2) People with a performer's mindset ask the question, "How can I do a good job?" When we're coming from this space, we don't want to be horrible, but we don't want to be great either. We often see what needs to be done to do a good job, but doing a great job seems like too much work, too much effort, too much stress. Doing a great job would be exhausting, and doing a good job is good enough.

3) High performers ask the question, "How can I be the best?" We love having these people on our team. We like to think of ourselves as these kind of people. When we ask this question consistently, we usually rise quickly in organizations, we win often, and companies that have these types of leaders asking the question "how can I be the best" often drive the companies or communities to greater heights.

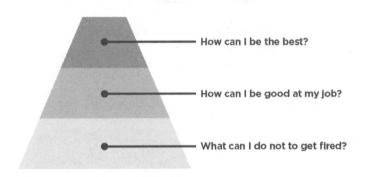

A caveat: At any given time, any leader can be anywhere on the performance pyramid. I can start a meeting in a high-performance mindset, get bored, and drift into a low-performance mindset and then end up in a typical-performance mindset, all in forty-five minutes or less. A high performer can drop into a low-performance mindset, and a low performer can instantly pop into a high-performance mindset.

It all depends on the questions they're asking.

Now it's probably self-evident that in the model above, the object of the game is to become a high performer. In fact, most leadership consultants will tell you that the object of the game is to become a high performer and to develop high-performing teams. Much ink has been spilt—and zeroes and ones have been coded—writing about high performance, how to become a high performer, and how to build high-performing teams.

But this should not be the goal, and we're about to see why.

THE HIGH-PERFORMER PROBLEM

Several years ago, I did some informal consulting with some leaders from a Fortune 10 company that would change my life forever. They were having some challenges with some of their leaders, and I asked them to describe what they thought the problem was. I was shocked when the first thing they said was, "Well, we're a group of high performers."

This surprised me because usually that's not the problem; usually that's the goal.

They were surprised too. They had never thought the very thing they were trying to create could be the source of the challenges they were facing.

So I asked them a question they had never been asked before: "What's the problem with being a high performer?"

"Well," they said, shifting in their seats, "It's like this . . ."

The conversation sounded exactly like what our coaches have

now heard from thousands of leaders in hundreds of other companies across the world. The leaders in front of me quickly rattled off a list of complaints about their high performers—and unbeknown to them, but more on that later—and it sounded like this:

→ They're resistant to feedback. This is because any feedback threatens their identity as a high performer.

→ They resent being asked to do more because they perceive their capacity as already maxed out.

→ They can become both simultaneously overwhelmed and bored. Overwhelmed because they feel like their plate is full; bored because they don't feel like they're growing.

→ They develop resentment from other employees who are not performing as well, but do little to help them.

→ They get jealous of others who surpass them—sometimes unconsciously conspiring against others' growth.

→ They're no longer coachable. They used to be, but now they don't think they need it.

This may surprise you, but simply knowing you can become the best makes you *less* likely to attain it. When high performance is the top of the pyramid, and you perceive yourself to be a high performer, then you have nowhere else to go other than to fall or protect your status as a "high performer."

Not only that but many people—even high performers—are actually afraid of being the best. For example, Jim Sherraden is one of the most famous printshop artists in the world. For over thirty years, he oversaw Hatch Show Print in downtown Nashville and has done work for everyone from CNN to Dave Matthews Band, from Emmylou Harris to REM. One time he told me an interesting story about what was going on beneath the hood of his performance. He was a wrestler in high school, and he talked about how he'd feel this gravitational pull away from getting first place during tournaments. Instead, he'd aim for third place. "Third place was good enough," he told me. "Good enough to be on the podium but not so good that you're the best." He called it "I am third" syndrome. It's a kind of "best" that hides untapped potential. High performers often long to be the best but are also afraid of being the best. So they get trapped in this tension without ever fully exploring their potential.

Both these psychological barriers—the arrogance of limited success and fear of the pain of success—are present but invisible, and consequently harder to deal with, in high performers and high-performing teams. The CEO of the Fortune 10 company who described the typical high-performance problem more or less said he had a staff full of prima donnas. High performers often act like Connor MacLeod in the TV show *Highlander*: "There can be only one."

Most people don't even see high performance as a problem. Even when I was working with the Fortune 10 company—a team full of high performers—I still asked the question: "So what's the problem?"

If you asked most organizations what they are trying to do, they would say, "Our goal is to create high-performing teams." But that actually might be a mistake. It's like saying your goal is to create a team of people who are a pain to work with. You can't be surprised when you accomplish your goal but then struggle to win. In sum, if you have a goal of creating high-performing teams, I want to suggest to you that even if you win, you lose.

> "If you have a goal of creating high-performing teams, I want to suggest to you that even if you win, you lose."

And that's when it hit me: I needed to upgrade the questions that high performers usually ask.

WHAT'S BEYOND HIGH PERFORMANCE?

To overcome these challenges, you must become obsessed with a question few leaders dare to ask: "Is there anything beyond high performance?" That question has become one of the driving questions of not only my life but our firm and institute and other companies.

Let me ask the question again: What's beyond high performance?

Our answer: meta performance.

Let's unpack this term a little because it's really important and because the term *meta* is used to mean a lot of different things.

Before it's popular use as "self-referential," or synonymous with virtual reality (and, of course, before becoming the new name of your most favorite or least favorite social network company), for thousands of years the Greek word *meta* had been used to describe the literal concept of "after" or "beyond." More than that, in the ancient world, *meta* took on a deeper meaning of transformation or even transcendence. Aristotle wrote his seminal work nearly twenty-five hundred years ago, exploring the ideas that shape philosophy and meaning and purpose. The title he gave his manifesto: *Metaphysics*. Five hundred years later, spiritual activist Paul of Tarsus wrote to a community in ancient Rome for people to be "transformed" by reinventing how people saw themselves and the world. The literal word he used: *Metamorphousthe*. Literary genius Franz Kafka published a book in 1915 exploring the bizarre experience of becoming something other than what was once before and titled his account *The Metamorphosis*—a name used by iconic artist MC Escher for his captivating woodcut prints in 1937 of forms slowly and seamlessly evolving into new forms. That word in particular has been used for centuries of modern science to describe the process of a biological organism miraculously transforming into something else.

So what comes after high performance? Or what literally means "beyond high performance"?

Meta performance.

So what does it mean? I'm glad you asked.

Meta performers aren't asking, "What's the least I can do?" They're not asking, "How can I do a good job?" They're not even asking, "How can I be the best?" No, meta performers are asking a fundamentally different kind of question. What motivates them and what energizes them and what shapes their careers and relationships and impact in the world is this question:

What am I capable of?

And since we know how the arrested effect works, we know asking this question compels a particular set of actions, and those actions are more powerful than those from the other three questions. When we ask, "How can I be the best?" that implies a finite answer or a limited subset of answers. You can actually be the best at something. You can be for the moment the best salesperson in your company (here's lookin' at you, Linda). You can be, for a moment, the richest person on earth (wink, wink Bezos and Musk). You can be, for a moment, the greatest basketball player to ever play (high five, Air Jordan and King James). The meta-performing question of, "What am I capable of?" on the other hand, has nearly *infinite* answers.

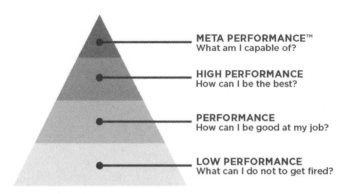

META PERFORMANCE™
What am I capable of?

HIGH PERFORMANCE
How can I be the best?

PERFORMANCE
How can I be good at my job?

LOW PERFORMANCE
What can I do not to get fired?

Turns out, human potential has fewer limits than human competition.

In other words, meta performers are never done. Not only do they have room to grow but they relish and create new opportunities to grow. They're in a constant state of becoming.

CHIK CHIK-A-BOOM, CHIK CHIK-A-BOOM, CHIK CHIK-A-BOOM

In 1933 a struggling actress going by the stage name of Diane Belmont was fired yet again from her gig as a chorus girl in New York City. During that same year, a young musician named Desiderio escaped with his family from the war-torn Cuba and found refuge in the United States. As a newcomer to this country, it didn't take Desiderio long to develop a thriving band that introduced America to the unique vibe of Cuban music.

In 1940 their lives crossed while working on the same movie set of *Too Many Girls*. He was leading the band, and she was one of the actors who was also hustling gigs on the side in comedy, dance, and radio shows. They instantly fell in love and quickly married before Desiderio enlisted in the military to fight in World War II.

It would be another seven years before this unlikely team—a fiery actress from New York City and a Cuban immigrant-turned-musician—would change the world of entertainment forever.

When Desiderio came back from the war, he and his bride wanted to spend some more time together. The best way for them to do that was to work together. So, partly in order to keep their marriage together, they developed a TV show about a married couple—to be played by them—and pitched it to CBS.

They got turned down.

In response, they took the idea on the road, performing in theaters across the country, testing out ideas, and proving that their concept of a Cuban husband and his redheaded wife could work. It didn't just work. It killed, and CBS was thrilled.

Of course, their story could have ended with them going back to CBS, selling the idea, and becoming talented actors on a great show. And that would be more than enough. But that's only the beginning. They didn't want to be *just* performers.

They wanted to explore what they were capable of. They didn't just want to act. They wanted to own the show. So even though their advisors tried to discourage them from the idea, they held firm, with Diane claiming to have been visited in a dream by a ghost of a friend who simply said, "Honey, go ahead. Take a chance.

Give it a whirl." They did. Instead of having CBS pay for their content, and thus owning it, the couple decided to start their own production company and finance the show themselves. They also filmed the show in a way that allowed them to resell and replay the episodes. This reselling and reairing of filmed TV content became known as "a rerun." They also invented the three-camera situational comedy ("sitcoms") filmed in front of a live audience—think *Friends* or *Seinfeld* or *The Fresh Prince of Bel-Air* or just about any other show you liked from the eighties or nineties.

Their show went on to become one of the greatest shows in the history of television, starring Desi Arnaz (shortened from Desiderio) and Lucille Ball, who had long since abandoned her stage name. Their show? *I Love Lucy*. And their inventions of the rerun and three-camera filming made them two of the greatest innovators in the history of Western media.

It would have been easy for them to ride the rest of their lives on the coattails of *I Love Lucy* fame and their technological innovations. That would have been more than enough. But they weren't done.

They wanted to explore what they were capable of.

So they took the profits from all their previous success and *bought RKO studios* from then owner Howard Hughes, renaming it Desilu Studios (a mash-up of Desi and Lucy). Desi ran the studio for several years after *I Love Lucy* went off the air and then eventually sold his shares to Lucille, who, as the first female president of a major production company, became the most powerful woman in Hollywood. Under her stewardship, Desilu created, among other shows, two obscure hits: *Star Trek* and *Mission: Impossible*. In the words of Desilu chief financial officer Ed Holly, "If it were not for Lucy, there would be no *Star Trek* today."[4] In 1968, thanks to her leadership, she sold a very profitable Desilu Studios to Paramount Pictures for $17 million—over $150 million in today's dollars.

And the rest, as they say, is history.

When you see J. J. Abrams executive producing the next *Star Trek* film, which currently has over a dozen movies—rivaled only by James Bond—and over eleven television series—rivaled by absolutely no one—or you see a fuse being lit and then Tom Cruise running, clinging to a plane, skydiving off a building or otherwise doing his own stunts in the *Mission: Impossible* franchise—seven movies and $3.5 billion of revenue in the box office and counting—you can remember it all is because of a Cuban immigrant and a redheaded firebrand who moved to Hollywood in the 1930s.

Desi went from being a refugee to a working musician to an actor to a writer and director and producer to media mogul. Lucille went from pinup girl to actor to writer to producer to studio executive and most powerful woman in Hollywood.

They kept asking the question, "What am I capable of?" They kept reinventing themselves—as artists, as business leaders, and as friends. Though their marriage ultimately ended, it wasn't their work that torn them apart. Ironically it was their work that kept them together. And though they divorced years before they died, Lucille was one of the last people Desi spoke to before he passed. They loved meta performance. They loved each other.

In my mind, few epitomize the meta-performing mindset like Lucille Ball and Desi Arnaz. They were people who consistently expanded their horizons to explore their capabilities. If they simply wanted to be the best—what high performers say they want, they would have stopped at *I Love Lucy*. But they didn't. They kept asking the ultimate question:

What am I capable of?

It's a question you can ask too.

META PERFORMANCE: A USER'S GUIDE

I was recently at an event where Netflix's former head of human resources spoke. She was one of their first thirty employees. She talked about infamous PIPs—performance improvement plans—and how people hated them because they were seen as a form of punishment or a legal paper trail so they could fire someone without getting sued. In most companies, people get put on PIPs when they're in trouble. During her presentation, I realized something about the culture of our firm and institute: every single person in our family of companies is on a performance improvement plan from the second they join our team to the moment they leave. We don't do this because people start "in trouble." We do this because we have a base assumption about people who choose to work with us: They all want to grow and improve. They don't simply want to be the best. *They want to constantly explore their capabilities.*

For example, every fourth quarter, we start looking at next year's goals and hold a space for our coaches to get clear on what they're committed to achieve. Our coaches can pick whatever goals they want, but they have to meet two criteria:

1. The goal has to seem improbable or impossible to them.

2. The goal has to be worth the cost of whatever it would take for them to grow to achieve it.

One of the greatest joys of leading the firm and the institute is seeing how year after year our coaches grow to achieve in December what they thought was impossible twelve months earlier.

That's the first step to becoming meta performing: create goals in which you're fully committed to paying the price to reinvent yourself and accomplish the impossible.

HOW IT FEELS TO DO THE IMPOSSIBLE

Years ago we were brought in to help a nationwide company close a $20 million budget shortfall. This is not a job for high performers. Usually, they think they're already doing their best, which is why they struggle to increase their performance. So overcoming this hurdle seemed impossible. This was a job for meta performers.

Our firm spent a year traveling the country working with their teams, doing two-day trainings and months of coaching with hundreds of their leaders, inviting them to see themselves as meta performers, upgrading their questions, and unlearning the "bad habits" of high performers.

At the end of the year, they didn't close the $20 million gap. Instead, they *surpassed* the budget by over $10 million. This is the power of meta-performing cultures. What was previously thought to be impossible becomes possible.

One of my favorite quotes from Walt Disney is, "It's kind of fun to do the impossible."

Most people think he's using understatement. We think, *Kind of fun? Are you kidding? I think it would be really fun to do the impossible.* That's because they've never done the impossible. To those who have never done the impossible, it feels daunting. To those who regularly do the impossible, it feels like any other day.

The greatest thrill of our work is when our clients tell us, "If you would have told us a year ago these would be the results we'd be creating, we would have told you it was impossible. But what we used to call 'impossible' we now call 'Tuesday.'"

That's what meta performers do. They turn the impossible into Tuesday.

So how do you constantly reinvent yourself—like the founders of the United States or John D. Rockefeller or Steve Jobs, Arnold Schwarzenegger, and Aaron Sorkin?

> → "That's what meta performers do. They turn the impossible into Tuesday."

How do you constantly push yourself to see what you're capable of?

I'll give you a hint that many high performers never figure out, let alone master: *you don't do it alone.*

 Want to go deeper on this topic? We've developed free resources for you and your team for each chapter, including discussion questions, recorded interviews with our coaches, and more. To access, scan the QR code or go to www.novus.global/book/chapter2.

CHAPTER 3
THE INEVITABILITY
OF OTHERS

Great things are never done by one person;
they're done by a team of people.

→ STEVE JOBS

Laughing to Death—Martin's Secret—What Navy SEALs Do—Funny F*t Guys—$1 Billion Brunch—Your Four Teams—Everyone Needs a _____—Playing a Bigger Game—The Genius of Inner-City Children

THE SECRET TO BECOMING
COMEDY ROYALTY

Pop quiz: Who has been nominated for a collective 238 awards, including Grammys, Tonys, and Emmys, and has won over 90 of them? Keep reading to find out (and why it matters).

In 2014 I was invited to see Steve Martin interview Tiny Fey about her book *Bossypants*.[1] The two were volleying punch lines back and forth, and at one point I was laughing so hard I actually started getting dizzy. They kept telling jokes, and suddenly my elation turned to panic. If I couldn't stop laughing, I was seriously afraid I was going to pass out. The world started to close in, and I began to slump against the person sitting next to me. I finally reached my hand out as if to say "Stop! Stop," and it nearly hit a man in the head who was sitting in front of me. Fortunately, Steve and Tina moved on to another part of her book, and I was able to catch my breath, and that's when I noticed that the man I almost smacked while gasping for air was none other than Eugene Levy from *Schitt's Creek*. Sitting beside him was Catherine O'Hara and Martin Short—all comedy royalty. As soon as I recognized who they were, I reflexively thought to myself, *What are they all doing here just hanging out? They're movie stars. Don't they have other things to be doing than watching an interview?* Flash forward to a month later, I got to be a part of a Q and A with Steve Martin and Martin Short for Short's new book *I Must Say*. This time I took my friend, who was a talented comedian and writer in his own right. During the evening, he raised his hand and asked them a question: *What was the secret to their success?*

First, they made fun of each other—this is what Martin and Steve do—but once they finally got serious we were surprised by their answer. No, they didn't spout off the usual clichés, like hard work, or make a joke about being really, really ridiculously good-looking. They simply pointed at each other, and then they pointed to a corner of the auditorium. And there sitting in the audience again was Eugene Levy and Catherine O'Hara and a whole crew of friends. Turns out, they love going to each other's events and celebrating each other's successes. Their answer was basically: each other. They weren't jealous of each other. Instead, they cheer and root for each other. If there was ever any competition, it was of the friendly variety. At one point one of them said, "We make each other better."

It got me thinking about a friend of mine, Brian Ferguson, a former Navy SEAL who is now a biotech entrepreneur. He took the best practices he learned as a Navy SEAL, along with his friend who is a fighter pilot, and turned them into principles for the people on the front lines of medicine. Since the pandemic, we've all become more aware of the importance of doctors and nurses taking care of themselves. One of Brian's passions is physical fitness, and he created a list of eight components that are essential for someone's overall health and fitness. If I were to ask you right now, without reading ahead, what he put as the most important aspects of fitness, what would you say?

Nutrition?

Cardiovascular exercise?

Strength training?

Sleep?

All solid guesses.

But when Brian did the research, the single most important factor that contributed to one's overall health and fitness was *community*. He argues change happens best when you intentionally design a community who values the same change that you do. Whether we're talking about twelve-step recovery programs, CrossFit, Navy SEALs, companies, or any sport, the reason why you're more likely to have success in these groups is you're not doing it alone. By creating an intentional community centered around a certain result, where there's accountability, some friendly competition, and mutual support—that is, rooting for each other, like Steve Martin and Martin Short were talking about—you will more likely commit to and achieve your goals.

Here's the answer from the pop quiz: Who has been nominated for well over two hundred of the most prestigious awards in entertainment? Not any one person. Martin, Steve, Catherine, and Eugene created that success together. They didn't do it alone. They did it as a team. See, they know what so many others don't: While they may be famous as individuals, they wouldn't be the meta performers they are today without each other—without showing up for and rooting for each other. All these comedians achieved greatness, went beyond what others had done, because they were able to unleash the secret weapon behind every meta performer. Turns out, there's a more powerful question than "what am I capable of?"

It's "what are *we* capable of?"

Put another way: meta performance is a team sport.

Sometimes high performers really struggle with this. "It would just be faster if I do it myself." I can't tell you how many times our coaches have heard this statement from our clients and each other. This is classic high-performer thinking, and at any moment we're all in danger of thinking this way. But I'm telling you: the second you begin to think this way, you've begun to decrease your ability to create in the world.

ALL ROADS LEAD TO . . .

I'll never forget when some colleagues and I were spending a day with some gifted high school students from underserved communities in Los Angeles. We had a theory that if the principles of our work were to be truly beneficial, they had to work everywhere, not just with the already uber successful. This meant we wanted to offer the same kind of tools to underresourced high school students that we gave to executives running billion-dollar companies and see what happened.

During the workshop with them, we talked about what would be extraordinary results they could create from our time together. Since these young people were in school, and grades are paramount in school, most of them said some version of, "It'd be extraordinary if I got straight As."

We pushed a little harder. "What is even bigger than you getting all As?" we asked. They struggled. In their minds, they had been taught their individual performance was the height of their ability to accomplish. Finally, after wrestling with the question for several minutes, one student raised their hand and said, "Something bigger than just me getting all As would be everyone in my class getting all As." And suddenly the lights in their imaginations went on.

"Imagine a class," one of them said, "that was like a group of Army Rangers, where they leave no man behind. Imagine if they committed to the grades not only

→ "All roads lead to teams."

meta-performing

of themselves but of their friends as well." That would require them to reinvent how they behaved in class, how they perceived themselves, and how they interacted not only with other students but even with teachers. For these students, shifting from all As to a classroom of As was a shift from high performance to meta performance. And that inevitably creates teams. It creates teams because you can't create a class that (ethically) gets all As without working together.

All meta-performing roads lead to teams.

Look around and ask yourself: *Who's on my team?* If you don't know, then we have some important work to do, and you're missing out on one of the most powerful performance-enhancing tools available. Another question I'd invite you to ask yourself: *Are you up to something big enough that warrants a team?* Not everybody is. And if you're up to something that can be done only by you, then your life is too small. Full stop. You are not made to be a part of something that can be done only by you. I want to invite you to broaden your vision about what is possible. We'll get to this more in chapter 5, but I want you to wrestle with this idea a bit right now. If you find yourself resisting the need for teams, then I want you to think of it this way: Meta performers expand their vision to where it requires other people to accomplish it.

High performers love working on their own. "I run fast, so get out of my way" they are tempted to think. Meta performers, on the other hand, eventually are up to something they can't do on their own. High performers often resist working with others because they're more aware of the costs of teams than the benefits. Sure, high performers can get tasks done on their own. They think they can do it faster—and more accurately—if they did it on their own. Yes, you can get a task done on your own, but you can't be a meta performer on your own. You cannot reinvent yourself on your own. Anybody who says, "I can do it faster if I do it myself," is the antithesis of a leader. The second you say this, you have abdicated your right to lead. You've heard the old adage—"If you want to go fast, go alone. If you want to go far, go with others." This is mostly true, but the whole truth is even better: ultimately you will *go both faster and farther* when working with teams.

But of course that doesn't always happen. Sometimes—maybe even most of the time—teams get in the way of growth. Not because of the problem of teams, but rather the problem of *team design*. Here's what I mean . . .

THE COMMUNITY'S ROLE IN YOUR REINVENTION

It's another one of the paradoxes of life that we crave both stability and change. If we have too much stability, our lives atrophy. If we have too much change, we have chaos. This plays out in community in profound ways because people are supposed to change, but oftentimes we want them to stay the same. Spiritual activist and theologian Timothy Keller once said about his wife, "I've been married to seven women, and all of them have been the same wife." This is human nature. They ebb and flow. Jungian Type Dynamics suggest that people's shifts and shimmies happen in a pattern. If someone is introverted, they sometimes go through an extroverted swing in their thirties and forties. If someone has been a raging extrovert for forty years, they may wake up and say, "I wonder what all this reflection is about?" and their lives change. This is normal. Change is normal.

Think about your team or primary relationships. Do you see them as fixed, static people, or do you see them as dynamic and growing people? We tend to have a need to see people as fixed because that's what's most comfortable for us. Even when they try and change for the better, we sometimes doubt their attempts at first because to see them as something new would require us to change how we see them, and that takes work.

Saturday Night Live has been around for forty-five years. And for nearly four decades, they used the overweight male comedian trope as a means to entertain. Everyone remembers the "fat guy in a little coat" bit made famous by *SNL* alum Chris Farley in *Tommy Boy* or his overenthusiastic motivational speaker who lived in a "van down by the river." Before Farley, there was John Belushi, and then there was John Candy, who hosted twice, and after him was Horatio Sans. *SNL* has always relied on the humor that comedians create with their size and shape. And if any of your friends were like mine growing up, you realize that professional comedians aren't the only ones using their bodies to make people laugh. I remember a friend of mine in college who adopted the persona of Chris Farley's "fat guy in a little coat." He leaned into it. He was smart, clever, silly, and embodied a kind of *SNL* comedic energy. And this worked for him, for a while. He made friends easily. People loved the archetype he was playing, and he was a genuinely nice guy. But I'll never forget the year when he came back from summer break. He had worked really hard through a variety of methods to lose over fifty pounds. What I remember now looking back was how our community reacted. You see, in class, he had spent years training everyone to see him as the "fat guy in the little coat." He was always the witty and sarcastic one.

One day, after losing all that weight, he spoke up in class to add to the conversation, and we all laughed, expecting what he said to be in jest. But I'll never forget the expression on his face. He had a look that said, "Hey, I'm trying to be serious here." He wanted to be taken seriously, but we hadn't gotten the memo. After all, he had trained us—and we had trained ourselves—for years to see him as the "Chris Farley" guy. Meanwhile, he was trying to say without saying it, "I'm trying to become someone else, guys." It was all subtext; nothing was ever explicitly said. He never had a public conversation with us about him wanting to change who he was. All this happened in the unspoken relating of our community. After all, we were all essentially kids and mostly not aware of what was even happening, or what to do about it. We didn't see, as a community, that we had a decision to make: Were we going to choose to see him as he used to be, or were we going to play a supportive role in who he was choosing to become? We all made a choice, whether any of us were cognizant of it or not. Eventually, he reverted to his old ways—at least while he was in college.

Fast-forward twenty years. After he left our college environment, he got a new job and a very successful career, a wife, and kids. He grew as a leader. He continued to take care of himself. His new world didn't see him the way his college peers did. He found a new community—a team, if you will—that supported and encouraged his emotional and physical well-being and health. He never lost his sense of humor, but he let go of the things that kept him from being who he wanted to be and created a new community that supported him toward that end.

On the opposite spectrum of my friend in college, you have the actor Matthew McConaughey. At first glance you might think these two men have little in common, but they do. For twenty years McConaughey made a fantastic living acting in shirtless rom-coms—*The Wedding Planner* with Jennifer Lopez, *How to Lose a Guy in 10 Days* with Kate Hudson, *Failure to Launch* with Sarah Jessica Parker, *Fools Gold* with Kate Hudson again. You get the idea. He had trained the world, successfully and lucratively, to look at him as a smooth, smiling heartthrob. But then one day McConaughey decided he didn't want to do that anymore. In his words, "I laughed louder, cried harder, loved bigger, loathed deeper, and felt more as the man in my life than in the characters I was playing in the movies . . . I wanted to . . . play characters that at least challenged the liveliness of the man I was."[2]

So he called his agent and said, "No more rom-coms."

And then he disappeared for two years. In Hollywood, that's a lifetime. Offers came in. One studio offered him $5 million for two months of work on a typical rom-com.

Pass.

They came back: $8 million.

Pass.

Then $10 million. Then $12.5 million. Then $14.5 million.

Pass.

Then, two years later, an offer came in for him to play a shady lawyer who works out of his car. From his book *Green Lights,* he writes: "Casting Matthew McConaughey as a defense attorney . . . was now a fresh thought. Going to McConaughey for the lead in *Killer Joe* was now a novel notion. Richard Linklater called me for *Bernie.* Lee Daniels came to me for *The Paper Boy.* Jeff Nichols wrote *Mud* for me. Steven Soderbergh called for *Magic Mike.*"

What was McConaughey doing? He was retraining people how to see him. He calls it "unbranding."

And then in 2007, he won best actor at the Academy Awards for *Dallas Buyers Club*.

Unbranding accomplished. McConaughey had successfully retrained people—agents, producers, directors, and his global audience—how to see him in support of who he wanted to become. Too many people try to grow without taking into account the retraining of their community it will require in order for them to become who they long to be.

There are two ways to relate to the two stories above: The first way is to ask yourself if you are in the kind of communities or team that is going to support your growth and are open to relearning how to see you. But just as important—and I'd even say more important—is the opposite perspective: healthy teams and communities aren't just about whether you're in the right community for *you* but whether *you* are the right kind of community *for others*. You can read the above stories as my college friend or Matthew McConaughey. Or you can read those stories as their friends, agents, and teammates. Are you like me and my college classmates, expecting our friend to stay the same when he was showing us that he wanted to be different? Or are you the kind of person who comes alongside of those wanting to grow to help them along the way? Of course, it's your responsibility to design a community that brings out your best. But one of the best questions you can ask yourself daily is: *Am I the kind of person who brings out the best in others?*

This is the great responsibility and opportunity of teams.

THE FOUR TYPES OF TEAMS

When my nephew was sixteen, I told him one of the most important things he needs to understand is that life isn't about *having* community; it's about *being able to create* community. Having community is passive. You have friends when you're younger and essentially have nothing else to do, and the whole world seems designed for you to meet new people. But then you get a little older, then friends move away or get married or have kids or maybe even die. Or maybe you move away or get married or have kids. Either way, as people age, their community often grows smaller and smaller. While this is true for a variety of reasons, there is a solution: never lose the ability to create new friends. If you become great at fostering and creating friends, then you'll always have community. It's so important for every human being to learn how to create community. It's not like riding a bicycle. Creating community is like speaking a language. If you don't use it, you'll lose it.

→ "It's so important for every human being to learn how to create community. It's not like riding a bicycle. Creating community is like speaking a language. If you don't use it, you lose it."

And just like creating community, it's important to learn to create teams as well. In order to fully step into meta performance, you'll need to design a community where you can bring out the best in each other. And one team isn't enough. In reality, there are *four* sets of teams every aspiring meta performer needs:

1. **The Team You Work For.** I've really benefited from the wisdom of Patrick Lencioni and the people at his consultancy firm, the Table Group. In Lencioni's book, *Silos, Politics and Turf Wars*, he talks about your "first team." Your first team isn't the team you lead; it's the team you're on. If you report to a board, your first team is the board, and your second team is the team you lead, the executive team of your company. Put another way: your first team is the team in which you follow somebody. And everyone follows somebody. Twentieth-century philosopher René Girard mused that the thing that informs what we want is the example of those around us. Everyone imitates. Everyone follows. Everyone is being influenced by someone. So it's important to answer these three questions around following: First, do you know who is influencing you (a.k.a. do you know who you're following)? Second, is following them getting you where you want to go? And finally, are you following well? Most of us, even high performers, have a boss or a manager or a supervisor or someone to whom we report. Even if we run our own businesses, we often have clients, people who pay us for our work and who need to be happy about our work in order for us to keep getting paid by them. It's important to learn how to follow well. At the Meta Performance Institute, we have a certification in coaching. We're working on a degree for leadership and management, and we've been talking about having a degree for followership. Followership is a lost art, and it is the key to becoming a great leader. To be a great leader, you need to be a great follower. I realize that might be counterintuitive. It's not what most of us are used

to hearing about what a leader should be. But if you don't know how to be on a team and to help bring out the best in others, especially those who are leading you, you will never be a successful leader. Most people try to skip this part. Everyone has a team they work on.

2. **The Team You Work With.** These are your peers, your colleagues, even your friends. These are the people you partner with and collaborate with and work and even play with. One of my favorite stories about this kind of team is from 1994 at the Hidden City Cafe in Point Richmond, California, where four friends named John, Andrew, Pete, and Joe sat down to have lunch and brainstorm about what they could accomplish together in the world of entertainment. They were all aspiring filmmakers, but at this point in time they hadn't put out a single movie. They were still in production with their first film; they didn't know if it was going to be any good, and it wouldn't be finished for another year. All the same, with the bustling clamor of the café in the background, they pulled out some pencils and started sketching on napkins various story ideas they thought might be interesting. Joe remembered a fable from his childhood about ants and grasshoppers. Andrew tossed out some ideas about fish underwater and robots in space. And there was some conversation about a unique take on monsters under the bed. They ended up with four concepts they thought were pretty good. And those four stories ended up generating over $2 billion in box office revenue. Joe Randt, Pete Doctor, Andrew Stanton, and John Lasseter—all producers

and writers and directors at Pixar—went on to become some of the most successful storytellers in history.

Not bad for one lunch.

Later, Stanton told reporters, "There was something special that happened when John, Joe, Pete, and I would get in a room, whether it was furthering an idea or coming up with something, we just brought out the best in each other."[3] Since that legendary lunch, Pixar has become one of the biggest and most awarded and acclaimed studios in cinematic history. Since its inception, Pixar has brought in nearly $15 billion worldwide. What happened between those men went beyond their individual abilities as artists, visionaries, and creators. For when brought together, they created something transcendent. Steve Martin, Martin Short, Eugene Levy, and Catherine O'Hara are prime examples of this. They didn't necessarily report to each other. This is just the natural kind of community you exist in to either work or live your life. It's important to learn how to partner well in your community for mutually shared goals. These are environments where there are no clear hierarchies or lines of authority. This is the jazz ensemble of your life (more on this in chapter 10). In jazz, it involves both leading and following. How are you at both?

3. **The Team That Works for You.** In business, this is the team you lead or manage. This is what most leaders think about when they think about teams—the team they perceive

as having the most authority to influence and contribute to—and so we won't spend much time on it here. One note worth mentioning is that oftentimes people don't feel like they "have" a team that works for them. But this team includes anyone you pay for anything. Mowing the lawn. Doing your taxes. Cleaning your home. Cutting your hair. Serving you at a restaurant. Serving you in Congress (#taxes). These people, if only for a moment, are working for us. They're on our team. Sometimes we're tempted to objectify them and their services, but this is a missed opportunity for growth. For we can also see them as more than just providing a service and see them as people to lead well and invest in and maximize. And, of course, if we work with them day in and day out, it's even more important to learn how to lead them well (more on this in chapter 8).

4. **The Team That Works on You.** When most people think of teams, they think about the teams they work on but not of the team that works *on them*. But the team that works *on you* is one of the most important teams you'll ever create. People in physical fitness know this. People who are the most successful in business know this. It's the secret of every successful individual: they had a team that was working *on them*. It makes me think of Eric Schmidt, one of the most successful CEOs in the world. Years ago he was winning. His team at Google was killing it. Then one day his board said to him, "We want you to work with a coach."

He asked, "What did I do? What's wrong?"

And the board said: "Nothing. That's why we want you to work with a coach." Schmidt was skeptical at first. But then over time he discovered the power and wisdom of having people invest in you and work "on" you as a leader and human being. Today Schmidt famously says, "Everybody needs a coach." He benefited so powerfully from coaching that he cowrote a book that distilled all the lessons he learned from his own coach titled *Trillion Dollar Coach: The Leadership Playbook of Silicon Valley's Bill Campbell*. Campbell famously coached Steve Jobs, Mark Zuckerberg, Jeff Bezos, and Schmidt. All those guys created billion- and trillion-dollar companies, and they did it because they worked to maximize all their teams: the teams they led, the teams they were on, the teams that worked with them, and the teams that worked on them.

What I love about having a coach or a team working on me is that they can see what I can't. You need someone outside your own mind to help you troubleshoot things that are mysterious to you and obvious to everyone else. *Metacognition* is an awareness of your own thought processes and understanding the thoughts behind them. If we want to become aware of our thought processes—and their limitations—we need someone to show us the way. There would be no six championship rings for Michael Jordan without coach Phil Jackson, who has thirteen championship rings. Jackson created and fostered the iconic Bulls team. Of course, Michael Jordan is the name that swallows all the other names on the team. But everyone knows that if it wasn't for Phil Jackson, that team would have never been what it was. Phil intentionally ushered

Michael into thinking about "we" versus "me." He was able to see things that Michael, Dennis Rodman, and Scottie Pippen were not seeing on their own. The transcendence of the game was facilitated by a coach who had a value explicitly for transcendence—and moving beyond "me" to "we." Even the Eric Schmidts, Michael Jordans, and Jeff Bezos of the world need other people. All the most successful people create, foster, and constantly develop teams that work with, on, and for them. We say it this way: in the video game of life, everyone has the next level, and no one gets there by themselves.

YOUR 4 TEAMS	YOUR ROLE	THEIR ROLE	YOUR SKILL	DANGER
TEAM 1: YOU WORK FOR	Employee	Employer	Following	Sheep
TEAM 2: YOU WORK WITH	Colleague	Colleague	Collaborating	Mob
TEAM 3: WORK FOR YOU	Employer	Employee	Leading	Tyrant
TEAM 4: WORK ON YOU	Coached	Coach	Growing	Saint

A QUESTION MORE POWERFUL THAN WHAT AM I CAPABLE OF?

During the 1991–1992 season, Michael Jordan won the MVP for the third time. In that year, he averaged 30.1 points, 6.4 rebounds, and 6.1 assists per game. He was so spectacular on both sides of the court that Bulls point guard B. J. Armstrong observed in the docuseries *The Last Dance*, "I felt Michael Jordan never played basketball anymore . . . he was just playing a different game than the rest of us." No, Michael—the Bulls—weren't just playing basketball anymore. They were playing a different game altogether. And that's what meta performers do. They transcend the game they are playing as individuals when they come together for a common goal. When you are with a winning team, all dedicated to lifting each other and plugging into each other's energy, you're not just playing a regular game anymore. You're not just a team anymore. You have transcended the game.

When you dare to ask, "What are we capable of?" you begin the act of transcending beyond high performance. You move into meta performance. And what is a meta-performing team's most important job?

The curation of a meta-performing culture.

 Want to go deeper on this topic? We've developed free resources for you and your team for each chapter, including discussion questions, recorded interviews with our coaches, and more. To access, scan the QR code or go to www.novus.global/book/chapter3.

CHAPTER 4
DESIGNING THE WIND ↓

To merely observe your culture without contributing to it seems very close to existing as a ghost.

→ **CHUCK PALAHNIUK**

Lessons from Terminal Velocity—What Teams Make—The Kansas City Chiefs—Yelling at Movie Screens—Lazy Rivers —Myers-Briggs—Questions the Wind Asks—How to Tend to the Garden

The wind screamed past my ears as the plane door opened at twelve thousand feet, exposing nothing but miles of empty space, clouds, and the distant curvature of the earth. This was my first solo jump, and I was doing my best not to think of the dozens of very plausible ways I could die in the next five minutes. Jumping by yourself out of a plane for the first time is just as terrifying as you might think. Sure, I had jumped "tandem" before, with professional jumpers strapped to my back who were as highly incentivized to survive the jump as I was. I'd jumped tandem out of planes in three different countries on two continents and even jumped out of a helicopter in Australia, but jumping out of a flying object at twelve thousand feet with *no one strapped to you who knows what they're doing* is a totally different experience. You have to train for it, and one of the interesting things about training to do a solo jump is that they call you a "pilot." When I first heard that I thought, *Pilot? I'm jumping* out *of a plane. I won't be* piloting—*I'll be* falling.

But then they taught me something I had never thought of before: you actually are piloting your parachute. Once your chute opens at five thousand feet, you have about five minutes to land in the right place, in the right way, with wind and elements doing their best to make that difficult. People jumping out of planes obsess over the wind. If it's too windy, you don't jump. And, of course, when you're falling at terminal velocity (120 miles per hour), there's a lot of wind. The stronger the wind, even the slightest move of your wrist or turn of your ankle can send you into a wild spin. The woman who trained me talked a lot about the

→ "When you're on a team, there's a wind blowing."

wind. "Jumping out of a plane is easy," she said. "Landing on the ground is pretty easy," she said. Then she paused and said, "But it takes a while to learn how to shape the wind."

It takes a while to learn how to shape the wind.

This is true when we're jumping out of a plane. This is true when we're leading ourselves. This is true when we're on a team.

Have you ever tried to change something on a team or relationship, and it was harder than you thought it'd be? Have you ever tried to change something inside yourself, and that was hard too? That's because people and teams exist inside a broader context of something that's hard to put our finger on but is always present. We can't always see it, but we always feel the effects of it. Maybe you could say it this way: When you're on a team—and even when you're not—there's a wind blowing. That wind is the hard-to-see-yet-easy-to-feel invisible force, and it's a wind that affects, amplifies, or fights against every move you make.

Another word for this wind: *culture.*

WHAT DO TEAMS MAKE?

Think about the teams you're on—it could be a marriage, could be family, most likely it's a team at a company or a sport, or maybe it's a partnership between you and a coach or therapist. Once you've thought of one or more of the teams you're on, I want to invite you to look at those teams as a kind of machine, and like all machines, a team is a machine that makes *something.* If you think about it, all machines make something. A watch is a machine that makes you aware of time. A car is a machine that makes transportation. A movie is a machine that makes a story. So when you think about the teams that you're on or that you lead, ask, "What do we make?"

Maybe we're a team that makes community, or maybe we make financial alignment, or we make revenue through sales, or maybe we make marketing, or maybe we make leadership results. These are all different outputs that the machine of a team could be designed to create. But there's another thing that all teams absolutely create: no matter how you design your team machine, no matter what it creates, the first thing that all teams create is culture. Whether you realize it or not, culture is your team's first and most significant output. I say it's the most significant output because it's through the culture of a team that anything else gets done. This is why Peter Drucker famously said, "Culture eats strategy for breakfast." You can design your team machine to perfectly produce whatever you want: cars, community, cosmetics, cures for cancer, but if the culture isn't right, you won't produce *anything*. This is true of any family, relationship, team, or company. So the primary question isn't "what does your team make?" The primary question is "does your team culture help or hurt what you're trying to make?"

This is harder to answer than it may look.

Generally, high performers don't usually think about culture. They usually are thinking about their own performance or maybe the performance of others. Part of the goal of this book is inviting high performers into continually expanding their field of vision to include—and enjoy including—expanding their capacity to create positive change around them no matter what role they have. And I'm telling you, if you want to maximize your capacity to create in the world, you have to become an expert in shaping culture.

The challenge to the culture problem is that culture for most people is incredibly difficult to see and measure. In the early twentieth century, culture was mostly seen as ballet and fine art. In the internet bubble of the nineties and early aughts, culture was defined by Ping-Pong tables and bringing your dog to work. Sometimes it's talked about in terms of popular culture or the culture wars or whether a culture is toxic or not. But these don't really get at the core of culture. Culture, like family, can be hard to understand until you're out of it and into another. Many people didn't realize their family of origin was weird until they started spending time with other families. Usually, it started with thinking other families were weird, until they realized all families were weird. That "weirdness" people experience around other people's families is a glimpse into the differences of culture.

Culture is powerful. It is an invisible thing that shapes you and the world you live in. It can be a curse or a cure.

→ "Watches tell time. Cups hold water. Teams make culture."

Most people don't even think they act, behave, or believe certain ways because of culture. Yet culture is the invisible, unspoken rules that people take for granted, that everyone has, even if they are unaware of it, and that guides their lives. Put another way, culture is a set of primarily invisible beliefs that shape our behavior and produce outcomes we either want or don't want.

THE ANATOMY OF CULTURE

Culture exists everywhere. Schools, organizations, sports teams, even "events" have cultures. If you've ever gone to a fancy polo match or regatta, amid the champagne and classical music playing, you'll feel instantly out of place if you don't have a fancy outfit, hat, or cap on. Conversely, have you ever been to a professional football game? There's no champagne. There's no classical music. American football is a totally different kind of culture than polo. I'm originally from Kansas City, and Arrowhead Stadium is notoriously loud. It's so loud that it's triggered machines that measure earthquakes from miles away. Something happens when all these Chiefs fans come together. For example, years ago, I knew a guy named Tim. Tim was six eight and weighed over three hundred pounds. He was one of those "silent giant" types. But Tim also had season tickets to the Kansas City Chiefs. When you take the gentle giant of Tim out of Kansas City and put him at the fifty-yard line, something overtakes him. Some things predictably—one might say magically— happen. Tim's shirt disappears. And suddenly, everyone sees that his entire chest is painted. He and all his friends paint letters on themselves, so when they stand together they spell *Chiefs*. Tim knows all the cheers and chants. For the three or so hours of play, he (usually mild-mannered and quiet) screams at the top of his lungs as if he were going into some ancient battle himself.

No one "taught" Tim how to do this. Before the games, there were no classes on what to do or how to act. *He just knew.* He absorbed the cultural experience of the stadium and transformed accordingly. Imagine if I were to instantaneously beam Tim a la *Star Trek* out of Arrowhead Stadium into the Olathe Public Library in the small suburb where I grew up. In the library, there's one sound that captures the culture. Everyone knows what it means to put your index finger to your mouth and say, "Shhhhh." It's universal for: "Shut up, people are trying to read." Generally speaking, no one teaches you how to do this. There are no classes on how to behave in a library. When you walk into a library, and your brain works the way most people do, you know to be quiet. That's the power of culture.

Culture is shaping you, your family and friends, and your organization, whether you realize it or not. If you show me your culture, I'll show you your future. One of my friends, whose parents are Vietnamese immigrants to the United States, told me a story of how her parents took her to a homeless shelter when she was young. She volunteered there all day. You might think, *Wow, what a kind and selfless thing to do.* But her parents were up to more than just a day of volunteering. At the end of the day, they turned to their daughter and said, "It's either Harvard or be homeless." Her parents didn't just put the fear of God in her; they put the fear of poverty in her. It's no shocker she went on to Berkeley, earned her MBA at Harvard, worked in the White House, and last week texted me a picture with her having a conversation with Henry Kissinger. When you ask her about her success, she'll say it was, in part, cultural. Her parents fled to America as refugees after the Vietnam War. As the successful and educated were driven out of Vietnam as threats to the communist ideology, they wanted to make sure their kids had the best possible mindset to succeed as they entered a strange new world. When I interviewed TED Speaker and *NYT* bestselling author Dr. Sandeep Juhar, he introduced me to the phrase *immigrant mindset*, which reminded me of my friend's Vietnamese parents. His parents, too, had created a culture in their family where anything less than the absolute best wasn't good enough. They didn't want their son to waste all they had sacrificed for him. There was a common joke in his community: "There are three things you can be: a doctor, a lawyer, or a disappointment to your parents." He became a doctor. These messages can be explicit—as in volunteering all day and being told this is how you will end up if you don't work hard. Or they can be implicit—the sense or feeling that you would be "disappointing" an elder if you chose something different for your life. Either way, this is the power of culture.

Every culture has advantages and disadvantages. Every culture is either helping you or hurting you, depending on what it is you're trying to accomplish. Culture is moving you toward some kind of future, every day, whether you realize it or not. And every culture has its distinct differences that make them unique. It's not wrong to acknowledge them, and doing the work to recognize your culture helps you navigate it clearly and see what you may or may not be missing by going blindly along with them without any self-awareness. So culture is *this thing* that is nearly invisible and yet shapes everything around us. That's why we say culture is like the wind. And if you want to be a meta performer or create a meta-performing team, you have to be able to learn to deal with the wind.

PART 1: LEARNING HOW TO SENSE THE WIND (CULTURAL AWARENESS)

In order to create a meta-performing culture, it helps to develop a lens for being able to see the culture around you. It should be noted that there are probably endless ways to measure culture. But we're going to present a few here to help you continue to explore how teams are being built and whether the culture is designed to get the team where it's built to go.

Just like in chapter 2, where we explored the four questions people ask when they're operating in the performance pyramid, and just like in chapter 1 we showed you the four ways people relate to work, you can use those paradigms to begin to understand the culture you're creating with the teams that you're on or you lead. As an example: Is your team trying to a) do the least amount of work in order to win (low-performance culture); b) do a good job (performance culture); c) be the best (high-performance culture); or d) explore what they're capable of (meta-performing culture). Similarly, are you and the people you lead or work with relating to work primarily as a) prisoners b) mercenaries c) missionaries or d) athletes? These are powerful questions that shape the culture you're creating and participating in. These are a great place to start when you're beginning to listen for the cultural wind that is shaping the trajectory of your team.

Here are a few more questions to help get you thinking about culture:

1. **What gets rewarded and valued around here? (Really.)**

   Rewards can come in all sorts of ways—acknowledgments, gifts, public recognition, raises, and compensation. These are all obvious examples of rewards. But there are more subtle rewards as well, like getting proximity to the people in charge. Who is the most popular and why? Sometimes it's because of their skill, or the way they dress or look, or how they avoid conflict, or how (hopefully) they add value to the company. Sometimes we reward "bad" behavior. In some cultures, the people who complain get the most attention. Implicitly, those cultures teach that if you want attention (reward), then find something to complain about. Whatever you reward and how you reward it, that's a major part of your culture.

2. What's tolerated around here? (Really.)

Part of what shapes a culture is what we collectively decide to tolerate. A classic example is a company we worked with that had a high-performance problem because they valued talent over their capacity to work with others. As a result, they tolerated a salesperson who treated others poorly because they were putting up numbers on the board. Even though no one liked him, everyone "tolerated" him. If only winning gets rewarded, that creates a culture that says, "We can be jerks so long as we win." Truthfully, this is a great problem to have, but it's still a problem. Most companies have the opposite problem: The toleration of low performance. Or the toleration of avoiding conflict. Or the toleration of the person in charge not having to follow the same rules as everyone else. These are all tolerations that shape a culture.

3. What gets punished? (Really.)

Most leaders and teams don't think of themselves as punishing, but every culture has adverse consequences for certain behavior. For some teams, missing a deadline has consequences. For others, it doesn't. For some teams, talking too much has consequences. For others, talking too little will have consequences. Some cultures value risk-taking; others shun it. For some, being aggressive will get you in trouble. For others, being too passive will. In most cultures, challenging authority will put you in the doghouse. No matter what, we all have behavior we punish one way or the other. This is part of the wind of your culture.

4. What are your rituals?

Every culture has sacred rituals. Mantras. And most of our rituals we are unaware of. There are annual rituals, quarterly rituals, weekly rituals. But we also have rituals of how we treat each other. Maybe two people on the team have the ritual of avoiding conflict. Or maybe there's the ritual of laughing at so-and-so's joke, even if it's not funny, because they're in charge. Or maybe it's the daily ritual of getting frustrated with so-and-so and not doing anything about it. Think about what you do before a meeting. Or what you do right after a meeting. Or what you do on your way to work or what you do before you sit in front of the computer. These are your rituals. Then there's the recurring thoughts and beliefs you tell yourself throughout the day. These are rituals. "Hey, Bob!" "Hey, Susan!" "How are you?" "Fine! You?" "Can't complain!" "Great! See you tomorrow!" These are all rituals. You may have heard it said, "What gets rewarded gets repeated," but equally true is this: "What gets repeated is getting rewarded somewhere." There's a reward for every ritual you have (more on this in chapter 7).

5. What stories do you tell (and retell)?

Every team or company has stories they tell or retell. How my sister Amanda joined our firm is a story we tell and retell. It illustrates a principle we have at the firm: healthy people ask for what they want. Amanda and I got trained as coaches at the same time years ago, but she got busy raising her family while I got busy coaching in the workplace. A couple of years later, she took me out to lunch and said, "I'd love to join the firm." And I said, "I've been waiting for you to ask." She's since become one of our top coaches, working with some of the most famous people on earth and cofounding our Meta Performance Institute for Coaching. We tell that story to illustrate how people win around here and let them know that it's okay to advocate for yourself. Many of the stories in this book of our community we've told hundreds of times among ourselves and in trainings across the world. They're our stories, and we tell them intentionally to shape our culture.

6. What's the personality of your team or organization?

While I have mixed feelings about personality assessments, I've been through several personality assessment trainings: from DISC to Birkman to StrengthsFinder to Enneagram to Myers-Briggs to the Big 5. Our firm and institute even have our own version of a personality assessment, but more on that in chapter 9. If I had all the time in the world, there's a part of me that would definitely enjoy geeking out on all these all the time. I've even watched popular TV shows with my friends trying to guess which number or color or top-five signature themes or four letters the various characters on the show are.

But as easy as assessments like these are to treat people as fixed and static and sometimes ungrowable or unchangeable, there is at least one benefit to them: they teach us that other people see the world in dramatically different ways. And while this is less true with groups of people—you always want to be careful labeling groups as thinking or feeling the same way, as it invalidates the uniqueness of the individual—all the same you can usually look at the combined results of a team's personality assessments, especially of those "in charge" or those who are perceived to have power or those others want to be like, and begin to understand the culture of the team even if the team can't see it. I'll take two quick examples from the MBTI—and for all you MBTI junkies out there, spare me the emails about how I did this wrong; it's just for illustrative purposes. Some teams are much more introverted than others. Some teams are much more extroverted than others. Our firm has worked with some of the most successful sales teams in the world, and they are expressive, get their energy from being around people, and get anxious if they have to do something in isolation. Then we've worked with some of the best engineers in the world. The energy in the room couldn't be more different. Not only that but those two rooms will "judge" people who are different from them. Engineers will get frustrated with other engineers who are "too talkative" or "waste time hanging out with others" or are "too emotional." To a team of engineers, these traits aren't valued as much, and those values, for better or worse, shape the culture. Conversely, salespeople will typically reject people who withdraw from them, who need time away from them, who rub them the wrong way with their blunt questions and seeming lack of "emotional intelligence." In fact, both teams would define *emotional intelligence* differently. Engineers would define *emotional intelligence* as a luxury, and salespeople would define *emotional intelligence* as getting what you want while appearing likable. Another time I did a training with a group of therapists. They had no problems extroverting their feelings, unlike the engineers, but they struggled to execute, unlike the sales team. They defined *emotional intelligence* mostly as being empathetic. Since these three teams valued different things, they produced different types of leaders, which in turn created unique, though predictable, cultures.

Whatever your answer to these questions, this is (part of) your culture. And the culture is sustained and cocreated by everyone.

Even you.

PART 2: LEARNING HOW TO SURF THE WIND (CULTURAL ALIGNMENT)

Once we begin to see the culture our team or system or company is cocreating, we can begin thinking about ways to enhance, build on, or otherwise change for the better. Of course, before we start trying to change the culture within us and around us, we have to acknowledge that not every part of culture needs changing and also that changing culture, especially in a business, needs to be in alignment with the people who are running the business. Before we try and change something, it's important to ask how that change will affect the primary stakeholders of a community. A lot of leaders will tell you about the importance of learning how to harness or surf the wind—how to not step on toes, how to not bother anybody, how to work the system. And there's nothing wrong with this. In fact, sometimes when the wind is really strong, and your sail is really small, going with the wind is the best thing to do, lest it rip your sail to pieces. Learning to surf the wind is an important skill.

To be honest, I struggled with this early in my leadership journey. When I first moved to Los Angeles in 2003, I had the job of my dreams working for a world renowned nonprofit organization. As I spent more time in the organization, I saw things I wished were different. I saw things that, in my own mind, *should* have been different. And so I said so, usually in an abrasive or arrogant way, usually behind the backs of the ones who were responsible for leading the organization. In ancient parlance, this is called "gossip," and it's incredibly toxic. Besides, most of the issues I noticed were things that were my preferences that the organization didn't necessarily value. Other times they were things that the organization *did value* but weren't valuing it the way *I* thought they should.

Whether my observations were "correct" or not is beside the point. As a new leader, I was questioning everything, but one question I *wasn't* asking was this: Are my complaints in alignment with the goals and values and timing of the people who are leading the organization?

Put another way: Is there alignment between what I care about and what those who are in charge care about?

As you pursue becoming a meta performer and creating meta-performing teams, one question to keep coming back to is whether you have buy-in, alignment, or what coaches often call "enrollment" for the necessary stakeholders who will be affected by your desire to go beyond high performance.

→ "When we try to force change without the enrollment of other stakeholders, we more often than not create more damage than good."

When we try to force change without the enrollment of other stakeholders, we more often than not create more damage than good. Surfing the wind is an underappreciated art.

PART 3: LEARNING TO SHAPE THE WIND (CULTURAL ARCHITECTURE)

I grew up near a gigantic water park, and it had a ride called the Lazy River. I've found this is most adults' favorite ride in a water park. You sit there, and the current takes you gently along without a care in the world. What causes this gentle current? Well, there are jets beneath the surface of the pool pumping about one thousand gallons of water per minute that creates a current, moving you in a certain direction, whether you want to go in that direction or not. If you want to change your trajectory, there are only two ways to do so in a lazy river. One is to swim against the current, which is exhausting and excruciating, but sometimes necessary. The other is to *shift the trajectory of the jets*. The same is true with culture. Some organizations have a low-performance culture. Most have a performance or high-performance culture. Very few have a meta-performing culture. So I invite you to begin paying attention to your own culture. Where are the jets that are beneath the surface of the water taking your team or organization? Where are they taking your life? Is it a trajectory you're happy with? Aligned with? Or do you find yourself exhausted at the end of each day, trying to out-swim and fight the current you find yourself on? If your answer is yes, you need to consider redesigning the jets, which is what the rest of this book is about.

But before we get to that, I want to point to the bull's-eye of what we're trying to accomplish: the creation of meta-performing leaders and cultures. The shift from high performance to meta performance is a cultural shift. And like we've mentioned in part 1, to do that, it's not enough for you just to change your behavior. It's about leveraging the power of teams for you to cocreate a new culture together. Behavior can be manufactured. Behavior can be faked. *Culture is when it's in your bones.* The power of culture is not just a behavioral change. The power of culture is where ideas, thoughts, and actions spontaneously erupt out of you in ways that I, as an author, will not even be able to predict. After reading this book, you're going to find new ways of doing things, discover new behaviors, and you may even write to me saying, "Is this what you're talking about?"

And I'll say, "I would never have thought of that. But yes, that is what I'm talking about."

When you start to inhabit the mindset of a meta performer, you become an ambassador for better-performing cultures. You create excellence around you wherever you go because *it's who you are.* This means that the inverse is also true: if your team isn't "getting it," it's probably because you're not bringing it. Step one can't be ignored: You have to model it. You become the jet stream, influencing those around you. You become the power in which the jet stream changes. Then everyone else can ride your wave. The more people who move in that direction, of course, the more powerful your wave and your impact.

You may be thinking right now, *Jason, I am only one person. How can I change my entire team, organization, or culture?* I want to assure you math is on your side here. Erica Chenoweth, a political scientist at Harvard University, extensively studied civil resistance as a means for radical change. In her research, she found, not surprisingly, acts of civil disobedience were the most effective in social change. She analyzed hundreds of campaigns over the last century and found that nonviolent campaigns were twice as likely to achieve their goals as violent ones. But the most surprising part of her research was that she found that 3.5 percent of the population participating in the protests were required to bring about that change.[1] Just 3.5 percent! Over the history of humankind, small minorities have exercised an incredible influence upon our cultures and have changed them for the better (and worse). It doesn't take a lot. In many cases, the organization's leaders set the tone for the entire organization. Conversely, it only takes a small minority to change it completely.

BEWARE YOUR OWN INFLUENCE

If it only takes 3.5 percent of people to change a culture, I want you to think about what attitudes or mindsets or habits you have that you *wouldn't* want others to have. Years ago I had a friend who was a high performer, but I would argue he had a low-performance mindset. In other words, he often asked, *What can I get away with?* I never met anyone who worked hard to get a job at a great company, and then I never saw anyone more blatantly disrespect the position he worked so hard to get. It's incredible how fast entitlement grows. If another person starts asking, *Well, if he can get away with it, why can't I?* it won't be long for that 3.5 percent of people in an organization to change the entire culture of entitled low performers. And just the other day, I read a headline saying this same company had challenges with entitled managers. The bottom line is that you're creating the culture you're a part of whether you like it or not.

When I reflect on the mindset I had while working at the nonprofit, I can see how if everyone behaved like me it would have been very bad for the organization. All of us have to do the internal examination to see what we're bringing to every interaction, every hour of work, every meeting and reflect on whether we're helping to build a great culture or destroy a culture we don't like.

I want you to think about the kind of culture you have now in your organization. How do you want to help in its redesign? I say "redesign" because whether you like it, it already exists. You have a culture already no matter what. How do you move beyond high performance? How can you redesign it toward better outcomes?

Years ago we collaborated with a tech company that had a problem with their programmers. They would never hit their deadlines. Conventional wisdom was "programmers don't hit deadlines." That's a cultural belief, and it's a total get-out-of-jail-free card. They brought us in, and we invited them to ask the question, "What kind of culture is going to help us get where we all want to go?" Quickly, the programmers acknowledged their own contribution to getting in the way of their collective success. It's not that they were "bad" or "broken" or "wrong." It was simply that they knew greater success hinged on them reinventing how they related to deadlines. So we worked with them to increase the level of integrity with their teams, which I'll discuss in depth in chapter 10. Sure enough, the programmers started hitting deadlines. They moved forward faster than they ever moved before. Sure, they still miss deadlines now and then. But the percentage dropped from 100 percent of the time to 30 percent of the time. That's a massive redesign of culture. When new programmers joined the company, they quickly discovered that things worked differently there. And they either got on board or found some other place to work.

NOTICE THE WIND	SURF THE WIND	SHAPE THE WIND
Pay Attention	Agility	Vision
Ask Questions	Adaptability	Disruption
Learner	Maximizer	Innovator

THE NATURE OF CULTURE IS CHANGE

Culture is not static. Whenever someone new enters an environment, the system changes. You know that from being in a family. If a new sibling arrived, a parent left, or a grandparent died, just one individual affected the culture of the community. But what happens if that entire family moves to a new community, state, or country? The culture around them would be different and affect them as individuals and as a family. In an organization or a team, people will come and go. They will bring their personalities, perceptions, experiences, and, yes, familial, social, economic, ethnic, and religious cultures with them. Redesigning culture is a continuous process. It's tending a garden. You're constantly tending to the garden of the culture. There will be weeds you need to pull. There will be unexpected growth. There will be circumstances and changes beyond your control. It's a never-ending growing, living, breathing thing. So we always have to be alert to culture drift and redesigning the culture to get us where we want to go.

For example, one of the challenges for our companies is protecting our value for giving feedback (more about this in chapter 8). We tend to drift toward not giving feedback as robustly as we can. Over time, we tend to pull our punches and not be honest with each other or making feedback antagonistic rather than a form of advocacy. This is a culture drift for us. As a result, people talk about each other rather than to each other. All this is normal, but we are noticing it. The good news is, we have the tools to do it because we teach this stuff for a living. For us, the question isn't, "Do we have the skill?" The question is, "Do we have the will?" You need both to design culture effectively. So what did we do? We put ourselves through the same feedback workshop we take our clients through. We publicly admitted this was something we were drifting away from at our annual retreat, we assigned a leader to temporarily help us keep focused on cultivating new habits of asking for and giving feedback with a plan to reevaluate how we were doing three months later. We know that won't be the last time we'll do that. Drift happens. This is why the goal of culture design isn't to make the culture "fixed" and "perfect," but to develop the habits of awareness and readjustment to keep your culture moving in the intended direction.

By now, we know culture isn't just Ping-Pong tables in the rec room or even vacation-day packages. It's not about if you get to work remotely or whether you have to dress up to come into the office. All of that isn't culture but cosmetics. What constitutes culture is how everyone agrees to treat each other by being a part of the team or organization. It's about what's expected of each other and what you can expect *from* each other.

→ "The goal of cultural design isn't to make the culture 'fixed' and 'perfect' but to develop the habits of awareness and readjustment to keep your culture moving in the intended direction."

So how do you redesign your culture into a meta-performing culture? You need to take a multidox approach to the GO LIVE values.

And that's what part 2 is all about.

 Want to go deeper on this topic? We've developed free resources for you and your team for each chapter, including discussion questions, recorded interviews with our coaches, and more. To access, scan the QR code or go to www.novus.global/book/chapter4.

PART 2
GO LIVE—THE MULTIDOX APPROACH

In part 1, we looked at the tension that all us high performers face when it comes to our lives and leadership: How to grow ourselves without breaking ourselves in the process. How to burn brightly without burning out. We were introduced to the concept of "meta performance"—and how it can enhance our lives and leadership. We discovered that all meta-performing roads lead to teams and that a team's most important output is culture. Then I suggested that when people choose to be athletes in life, embrace a meta-performance mindset, lean into teams, and rally behind creating meta-performing cultures, amazing things begin to happen.

Part 2 is your compass for how to do just that. In the following chapters, we're going to explore the six values that generally make up the meta-performing mindset and create meta-performing teams and cultures. While we'll walk through each of these values one by one, don't confuse the order with a step-by-step prescription. I tried to put the values in an intuitive order—we start with vision, which is where most of our coaching starts with new clients and companies—I could have just as easily started with any of the other five values and gone on from there. We'll use the acronym GO LIVE (rhymes with "give"), which stands for growth, ownership, love, integrity, vision, and energy. But the order of the acronym isn't the order we'll cover them in this book; it's simply another tool to help you remember the values.

Before we begin, I want to explain a concept we care deeply about at Novus Global and the Meta Performance Institute. We take what I call a "Multidox Approach." To understand the term *multidox*, it's probably easiest to point out some other familiar *-dox* words and their meanings. First, *dox* means "beliefs." So *orthodox* means "correct beliefs," and *heterodox* means "different beliefs," etc. For our purposes, we're going to look at three other "doxes"—unidox, paradox, and multidox—and how they'll apply to the rest of this book.

Unidoxical Thinking: This is a linear way of thinking that invites little nuance. There's either the right way to do things or the wrong way. "I'm right, and the 'other' is wrong." For unidoxical thinkers, there are not two sides to every story. There is one side: theirs. The focus is on being right or on making others wrong. If they're looking at the picture below, they either see two faces or a vase. But they commit to only seeing one and will argue with anyone who thinks they see something different. They choose to see life through one lens. Pick a topic, and they'll find a way to bring it back to whatever they're passionate—or usually angry—about. One of my favorite quotes about this is from Winston Churchill: "A fanatic is someone who can't change his mind and won't change the subject."[2] That's unidoxical thinking. This kind of thinking isn't "bad" per se. But it is limited when overused, or when used exclusively.

Paradoxical Thinking: Paradoxical thinking is living between two tensions. It's not left versus right, but left *and* right. It's acknowledging the value (and costs) and synergy of seemingly contradictory values. For paradoxical thinkers, there are "two sides to every story." The focus is on balance. With paradoxical thinkers, they're able to see both the face and the vase, or—with the picture below—the bunny and the duck. (One interesting side note: it's nearly impossible for people to see both the duck and the bunny at the same time; notice how your mind switches back and forth). It's difficult to hold the bunny and the duck together at the same time, but as F. Scott Fitzgerald famously said, "The test of a first-rate mind is the ability to hold two opposing ideas in the mind at the same time and still retain the ability to function."[3] These folks are able to metaphor-switch, so to speak. As an example, they're able to see the pros and cons of two parties in a two-party political system. They can switch back and

forth between the Donkey and the Elephant (for the US system). If you ask them if they're conservative or liberal, they'll say, "It depends on the issue," or even "It depends on which level of government you're talking about,"[4] or even "It depends on who was in charge last and how they did," etc. There are benefits and weaknesses to this kind of thinking as well. No type of thinking is "right" all the time.

Which leads us to a new paradigm I'd like to introduce to you. Most of us live trapped in a unidoxical mode of thinking, and some of us are fluent in a paradoxical way of thinking. But in order for people to step into their meta-performing future, a more complex style of thinking is needed. We call this style "multidoxical" thinking.

Multidoxical Thinking: This type of thinking is dynamic. When we approach the values and principles in a dynamic system, we can hold all the values equally overall, but we emphasize one over the other at certain times. Multidoxical thinking is adding layers of dimension to paradoxical thinking. It's more than the synergy of two opposing viewpoints. It's looking at an issue from multiple—read two or more—vantage points and with the consideration of multiple factors. To a multidoxical thinker, there aren't two sides to every story. *There are way more than that.* It's the tension and interplay between those things that create beauty. Dan Leffelaar, from our firm, offers this analogy: "Each string in a piano creates a tension (two fixed points connected by a string—paradox). When you take all eighty-eight keys (and eighty-eight strings) in a piano, that creates around thirty-six thousand pounds of pressure. It's all those pounds of tension from these keys that create the possibility for all this beautiful music." Whereas in literature you're taught not to mix your metaphors, multidoxical thinkers love to mix their metaphors. Because it's in the mixing that a fuller picture of reality begins to emerge. Wherever two or more metaphors or viewpoints are present, multidoxical thinking is there. The image that can represent multidoxical thinking is a necker cube—itself a paradox developed in 1892 by a Swiss crystallographer—with two separate optical illusions on two of the six sides of the cube.

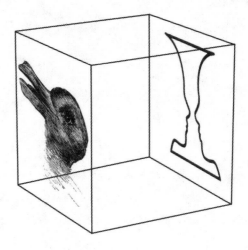

There are eight different *completely accurate* ways to see the above image:

1. a cube with a duck and vase

2. a cube with a bunny and vase

3. a cube with a bunny and two faces

4. a cube with a duck and two faces

And then perspectives five through eight double all the above since the cube can be seen in two different ways as well, with the larger left square either being in the front or the back.

	UNIDOXICAL	PARADOXICAL	MULTIDOXICAL
MOVEMENT	Static	Balance	Dynamic
ISSUES	One side	Two sides	Many sides
MUSIC	One note	Dyad	Chord
CONVERSATION	Monologue	Dialogue	Trialogue
VALUES	Single issue	Two values	Systems thinking
INSTRUMENTS	1x string	2x strings	2+ strings
SINGING	Solo	Harmony	Symphony
POLITICS	One party	Two Parties	Three+ Parties
POWER	Dictator	Monarch & republic	Checks & balances
MEDICINE	One opinion	Second opinion	Triangulate opinions
FURNITURE	Pole	Ladder	Stool

We want you to look at these next six values multidoxically. Look at the GO LIVE framework as paradoxes to mix and play with, to see the tensions and synergies as they interact and influence each other. Think of them like ingredients to your favorite meal. Each ingredient affects the others. Salt has a taste by itself, but it also brings out flavor in other foods. While each value contains paradoxes—you've got to get blind to see, you've got to rest to grow, you've got to let go to move forward, you've got to give energy to create energy, etc.—it's not just about understanding the paradox within the value but understanding how these values enhance or create tension or sometimes seem opposed to each other. You can play anything with these six "keys" or bake anything with these six "ingredients" or wrestle with each of these paradoxes to produce wisdom, because *it's how they interact with each other* that creates the music, not the keys or values themselves.

And you can't separate them. The ancient activist Paul of Tarsus wrote in the first century about how communities of people interact like a body interacts with itself. You've got all the various body parts: hand, feet, head, etc. None of them can exist independently of each other. He writes, "The hand can't say to the foot, 'I don't need you.'" It's the same thing with these values. They need each other to be most themselves. This is true for people. This is also true for values to be healthy. They find their fullest expression in relationship to each other. Imagine having a piano that only had the C note. You would have serious limitations on what you could play. Or imagine trying to bake a pie with only sugar. Or trying to live life thinking truth is found in only one point of view (#politics). You need all of them working together to achieve meta performance and go beyond what you currently believe you're capable of. For example, if you want to be physically healthy, it's not enough to just focus on diet. Or sleep. Or exercise. Or hanging out with other healthy people who will encourage good habits. You need to create a system of health that is mutually reinforcing—the paradox of exercise is that you have to get tired to have more energy. Of course, you have to start somewhere, but there's no "right" place to start with your health. The best place to start is the place where you're committed to starting. No matter where you start, the endgame is the same: eating right, getting plenty of sleep, regular exercise, and a community where all these habits are encouraged and normal. That's a system. That's a multidoxical approach. Health is an emergent property of a system designed to produce health. Pie is an emergent property of flour, sugar, butter, fruit, and heat combining in various ways. Meta performance is an emergent property of the endless tension and synergy of the following six values.

One last thing: Our six values aren't necessarily unique. I even had people on our team ask to come up with sexier words to describe them. Instead, I opted for clarity (after all, we already made up *meta performance* and *multidox*—I figured I'd give you a break on other made-up words . . . at least for now). What's notable is how they interact with each other in an ecosystem of values, with yourself, and with others.

Okay, enough of that. Let's look at the six GO LIVE keys and play some music.

CHAPTER 5

CREATING FROM THE FUTURE

The future ain't what it used to be.

→ YOGI BERRA

Blinding Speed—Everyday Visionary—You Gotta Want It—Coffee Filters— Your Late Great Childhood—Pattern Recognition and Window-Shopping—Plus Other Stuff

David Brown is the fastest man you've never heard of. In 2016, at the Olympic Games in Rio De Janeiro, Brown found himself standing on the center podium feeling the heavy weight of a gold medal placed around his neck. Booming in his ears was the roar of a stadium and the American national anthem playing. He had just set a *world record* for the one-hundred-meter dash. But there was something else that made his accomplishment even that more spectacular: he had just become the world's fastest *blind* man.

And David Brown knows a thing or two about vision.

HOW TO BE A VISIONARY

Most books on leadership and high performance include a chapter on "vision"—typically, they prescribe that to succeed you must have a "vision." The problem with this is that all humans *already have a vision*. All people are visionaries. This is not obvious to most of us, but if I were to ask you what you think your life will look like a year from now, you probably have an answer. Most people answer it like this: "More of the same." Others have timed markers of external events, like, "My kids will be out of the house," or "I'll have this new position at work," or "I'll be making a little bit more money." People who lead businesses have projected growth for their companies. "We'll grow by 15 percent this year." Whatever your answer is to that question is your vision because a vision is literally "what you see" about the future. So when I ask you what your future looks like and you describe it to me, congratulations! You're a visionary. All of us are. But even as all of us are visionaries, not all visions take us where we're meant to go. And one of the first steps we can take in increasing our vision for our lives and leadership is discovering what we can't yet see.

Before we can appreciate the power of vision, we first have to understand that all of us are in some ways blind. In leadership development, oftentimes these areas of our lives are called "blind spots." Everyone has them. No one can see all the data needed to make the correct decision every time. "Even our best decisions are always made with incomplete information." David Brown understands better than most what it means to have blind spots. When he laces up his shoes and places his feet in the running blocks, the most important sense that he needs to do what he's about to do is absent—he runs wearing a blindfold and tethered to a running partner to guide direction. And yet David is still able to accomplish his dreams of being a world-class athlete.

That's because having blind spots isn't what we think it is.

LEVERAGING YOUR BLIND SPOTS

"I want you to help me discover all my blind spots," a potential client once told me as we hopped on a video call for the first time. I remember his earnestness and passion and maybe even pride as he said it. He knew that most leaders vaguely understand they have blind spots in their leadership and that even fewer ever have conversations to address them, so he was expecting me to be impressed that he'd be willing to address time and money to help him. So you can imagine his surprise when I looked at him through the screen, smiled, and said, "No."

Shocked, he said, "Why not?"

"Well," I said, "First of all, there are too many, and that would take forever." This was a joke (but not really), and I was glad he laughed as I said it, meaning he took the joke in the way it was intended.

"Second," I continued, "Not all blind spots matter."

"Tell me more," he said.

"Well, right now, look around at what you can see."

He did. He was sitting in his office in Atlanta.

Then I said, "Can you see the Eiffel Tower?"

"No." All he could see was his office space around him.

"Exactly," I said, "You can't see the Eiffel Tower. Another way of saying it is that you're *blind* to Eiffel Tower right now. That's one of your blind spots. Worse than that, there's a lot you can't see: the Grand Canyon, what's on sale on Rodeo Drive in Beverly Hills, or how many people are currently outside the Cozy Inn in Salina, Kansas, waiting to get a burger (they have the best burgers). You can't see any of these things. You're in an office in Atlanta. But in your life and leadership, none of that really matters because none of those things are keeping you from getting where you want to go. If you wanted to get to the Grand Canyon or the Eiffel Tower or have a Cozy burger, that would be different. But you don't."

Blind spots only matter if they keep you from accomplishing your vision. The irony with Paralympian David Brown was that being blind *wasn't a blind spot*. Of course it's impacted his life in powerful—and painful—ways. And when I asked him if he could go back and undo the effects of the Kawasaki disease that stole his sight before the age of ten, he didn't have to think twice: "Absolutely." But when you ask him if being blind has kept him from achieving his vision of devoting his life to sport, he'll say, "Absolutely not."

In fact, the most successful leaders understand

→ "Blind spots only matter if they keep you from accomplishing your vision."

that blind spots don't necessarily keep them from accomplishing their goals. More than that, meta-performing leaders are intentional about what they're blind to. They are strategically blind, or what Steven Sample, the former president of USC, described as "strategic ignorance" in his book *The Contrarian's Guide to Leadership*. Like a horse at the Kentucky Derby, leaders put "blinders" on so they can focus on what's most important to them and shut out everything else so that they don't get distracted from the goals and dreams they long to accomplish.

Brown uses his blindness as a feature of his success rather than an obstacle to it. The reality is, even though Brown can't see, he is still a person of vision.

And in that way, we can all be like him.

ON FILTERS

If you want to maximize the value of vision in your life, you've got to first understand how you perceive what's around you and the connection it has to how you create meaning in your life. It's important to know that "perception" isn't a passive activity but a creative one. When you perceive, you're not just receiving data. You're also creating data. For example, when you look around, you're not really seeing what *is*. Most of what you're seeing is created from memory—you see what you expect to see based on what you've seen in the past. Think about how strange that is: when you look around at whatever room you're in, you're not seeing the actual room. That's way too much data to take in and would take too much energy. Instead, our brains seek efficiency, and so it is faster if the visual cortex does as little as possible, using filters to "cheat" or quickly determine which data to emphasize and which data to ignore. Your brain filters about eleven million bits of information down to about fifty bits of information every second.[1] That's some serious filtering. Which means we're not seeing reality as it is but as we filter it.

If this sounds unusual, consider the phenomenon of change blindness. Change blindness is where you look at something that is constantly changing, and you're unable to see what changed. There are several examples of this, but my favorite is when researchers went onto a college campus and interviewed students about some random topic, then, in the middle of the interview, two people carrying a gigantic door rudely walked between the interviewer and the college student being interviewed. While the student's view of the interviewer was obstructed by the giant door and the rude door movers, someone else came and *took the place* of the interviewer, so when the door finally passed there was a *totally different* person interviewing the college student.

The students often didn't notice any change.

This study illustrates how even if we're interacting with someone, we're just not that aware of what we're seeing.

There's a lot of information we're missing because we're mostly seeing what we expect to see. That's the filter of memory at work.

Another primary filter you have is the filter of desire. If you're looking for your keys, then you have a filter called "scanning for keys." You access from your memory what keys look like, and if you're lucky also where you remember putting them. As you search for your keys, you'll tend to ignore any information that occurs to you as "not keys"—even if that's where the keys are—all so you can focus on the information you want: keys. So then these two filters—the filter of memory (what I remember keys looking like) and the filter of desire (I want keys)—shape whatever data you allow your brain to process in order for you to find what you're looking for. At any given moment, memory and desire are two (among others) default filters creating what you call "seeing." These filters don't show you reality in totality, but your filters decide what to focus on and what to ignore so you can create a useful picture of reality in your head. These filters combine to help you move throughout life, but here's the important thing for this chapter: these filters mean there are parts of reality that you're not seeing.

Not only that—we also think we see things that are not there. Below is a quick-and-easy exercise about how your mind takes what it finds and sees meaning that isn't really there. Do your best to read the (obviously misspelled) text below:

It deosn't mttaer in waht oredr the ltteers are in, the olny iprmoetnt tihng is taht the frist and lsat ltteer be at the rghit pclae. The rset can be a toatl mses and you can sitll raed it wouthit mcuh of a porbelm.

Even though the letters are mostly nonsense, most people are still able to create meaning from the letters above. This is because, as you look at the lines on the page, you have memory of how words are spelled and memory of how sentences are usually structured (filter 1), and your mind also has a desire to take lines that we call "letters" and make sense of them (filter 2). So memory plus desire creates a filter that transforms the sentence above into something like this:

"It doesn't matter what order the letters are in, the only important thing is that the first and last letter be at the right place. The rest can be a total mess and you can still read it without much of a problem." That, of course, is not what it said, but it is what we *read*. It wasn't the content, but it was what we created.

Where this is most relevant isn't necessarily when we're looking for keys or observing colors in a room or reading misspelled words. It's most relevant when we're imagining our future. Because if our filters are hiding parts of reality from us, that means it's hiding futures from us too.

ORDERING FROM THE MENU WE SEE

In my twenties, I moved to Los Angeles and discovered the fast-food burger joint In-N-Out. Aside from having great food, an admirable company culture, and my favorite french fries, In-N-Out is famous for having a *very* simple menu—in contrast to a restaurant like the Cheesecake Factory, which has a menu longer than Dostoyevsky's *Crime and Punishment*. There are only a few things you can order at In-N-Out, and they're all delicious. So when I go there, I always get a double-double burger, animal style, fries, with tea to drink (and maybe a chocolate shake). No problem. I like that the menu is limited; it makes making decisions on what to eat a lot easier. Our brains work much the same way as an In-N-Out menu. We get overwhelmed if we have too much choice (what psychologist Barry Schwartz calls "the paradox of choice"—the fact that we want options and yet get overwhelmed by too many of them).[2] Like we've mentioned earlier, our brains uses filters to limit the options on our menu to make it more like In-N-Out and less like Cheesecake Factory. So long as we use the same filters, our menu stays the same, and so long as the menu stays the same, we order the same thing. This creates what leadership experts and authors Steve Zaffron and Dave Logan of *Three Laws of Performance* call a "Default Future."[3] A default future is what will naturally be created if our "menus" stay the same. For example, let's say someone hurts me during a conversation, and the only available options I see on my "menu" of responses are

1. yell at them, or

2. shut down and withdraw.

If these are my only two options, then I'll usually order a number two with extra shame until I can't stomach it anymore, and then I'll order a whopping supersized version of number one, animal style. I behave this way because they're the only two options I have on my menu. But my menu isn't a reflection of all available choices. Most people, including me, recognize this, but it doesn't change our menu. My menu is a representation of choices that my filters allow me to see. That limited menu limits our choices, which in turn limits our future, since our future is created by the choices we make today.

In this way, we have filters about everything that limit and shape our choices.

We have filters about ourselves.

We have filters about others.

We have filters about work.

We have filters about money.

We have filters about God.

We have filters about power.

We have filters about what's possible.

We have filters about everything.

And we treat these filters *as if they're reality.*

Most people are unaware of their filters. We have them, but we don't realize we have them. In coaching, when we're unaware of our filters, we don't say we have filters; we say *our filters have us.* When we become aware of our filters, they can become a tool we can use to create what we want with our lives and leadership. When we're unaware of our filters, they are a cage we can't escape. It "has us." When a filter has us, it limits our agency because we can only see possible futures that the filter allows us to see. We'll talk more about how to discover your filter and how to take responsibility for it in chapter 7. But for right now I want to ask you this question: What is influencing your filters? What are you allowing to shape what you see for you and those you lead?

Let's go back to In-N-Out for a minute. I'll never forget the time I went there with some friends, and they ordered something that *wasn't* on the menu. I looked at them in shock, and

→ "When we're unaware of our filters, we don't say we have filters; we say our filters have us."

before I could say, "That's not on the menu," the person behind the counter smiled and said, "Absolutely. Coming right up." Turns out, In-N-Out has a *secret* menu.[4] You can only order off the secret menu if you know about the secret menu. I think about this moment almost every day as it pertains to my future and the future of our clients and the people training at our institute. Your perception of the future is like a food menu. When you're living in your default future, you're just ordering from the options readily available on your menu. The challenge with this is that there are potentially more desirable futures that aren't on your menu. You can't see these potential futures, because they've been deleted by your filters. And you cannot create a future you can't see. Here's the truth: there are futures completely possible for you that you are currently blind to because of the filters you are using in your life.

We say it this way: our filters influence our future.

YOUR FUTURE FILTERS

Now here is what's exciting about our filters: they are not unchangeable. It's not like we have to keep our menu the same or have to keep looking for keys or interpret "waht" as "what." In fact, many, if not most, of us have experienced the moment when we learned some new information or had some new experience and—unknowingly—shifted our filter, which changed how we saw reality. You see, we have some degree of choice in which filters we develop and which filters we discard. And if it's true that we choose our filters, then it begs the question: Which filters should we be choosing?

If I change my filters, I change my future. That's because there are paths to the future that can only be seen with certain filters. The future you desire shapes what you allow yourself to see in the present. If you want to get from Los Angeles to New York City, in the present, you won't care or notice highways that take you to Seattle. Those will get filtered out. In the same way, if you want to get from Los Angeles to New York City, but your menu doesn't include "flying in an airplane," then your present will be full of planning a weeklong road trip versus one day in an airport. But as soon as you say you want a future that gets you from LA to NY in one day, then immediately driving is out and you have to find another way to create that future. In this way, it's not just the present that determines our future but our future that determines our present.

Put another way: our future can influence our filters.

This is what Steve and Zach call a "Generative Future." A Generative Future is where we begin looking first for a preferred future and then begin exploring "off-menu" possibilities to create that future. This is the way meta performers learn to think about vision. They start with a filter for a deeply desired future and then allow that vision to inform how they see the present—and even their past.

So how do we do this? It starts with where the future meets desire.

THE LANGUAGE OF THE FUTURE IS DESIRE

There is a transportation device that moves all people from the present to the future. It's that thing we mentioned earlier called "desire." Right now you're doing whatever you're doing because it's giving you something you desire. We go to work because we desire the things that work gives us. We put down our book to do something else because there's something else we want to do more than read a book. Whatever you're doing today is the result of whatever you desired yesterday. We know what people want based on the choices they make. Every time we make a choice, there is desire at play, and often those desires we are not consciously aware of. When our coaches are working with leaders and teams to begin capitalizing on the power of vision for their lives, we over and over again bring them back to the language of desire:

What would excite you?

What would thrill you?

What do you want?

What do you long for?

When you're thinking about your role in a company or your leadership in any area of life, you want to develop a picture of the future that excites you, that pulls you forward. Just like filters, some people don't have desires; sometimes desires have people. The difference is whether you are aware of the desires that are driving your current behaviors, habits, goals, etc. The object of the game is to design a future that pulls you into the future versus a future that you avoid or a future that you have to strain to move toward. In the best of situations, you're looking for a future that creates new compulsions that you can trust.

Of course, some people are committed to *not* being excited. Being excited can be vulnerable, and often high performers avoid getting vulnerable at all costs. One time I was talking with a client, and they said, "Jason, I just don't get excited about very much anymore."

And I said, "That's interesting. How long have you been committed to not being excited?" For most of us, it's not that we *can't* get excited; it's that we don't *want* to be excited.

But if excitement leads to a dead end for you, we can try the word *passion* instead. The word *passion* means "to suffer." You know what people are passionate about by what they're willing to suffer for. Any time you meet someone who says they're struggling with passion, just follow their suffering. As strange as it may seem, many people are suffering most from an acceptance of mediocrity in their lives. Which means what they're actually passionate about is . . . mediocrity.

Either way, what you're hunting for is a vision of the future that lights you up. You know the old saying: "What would you do if you knew you couldn't fail?" This might be a good place to start. This question creates a freedom to play and say seemingly ridiculous things. But as I reflect on the choices I've made over the last twenty years of my career, I realize my best moments weren't spent living the answer to that question, but a better question. For years now I've been asking myself the question, "What would you do if you knew that you would fail, but you'd do it anyway?" The first question is about freedom from failure. The second question is about freedom to transcend failure. The first question is about certainty. The second question is about passion. Both are helpful in deciding which future you want to be your filter.

BACK TO THE FUTURE

This is the most important idea for you to get from this chapter: once you get a vision for the future that excites you, now you can leverage that future *as a filter* to begin interpreting the present to help you achieve that vision. In other words, you start creating *from the future*. Your desired future becomes your dominant filter. I want to invite you to picture this almost literally: imagine you're holding a lens of the future and then you lay it on top of your present. When you do this, it's going to emphasize certain data and minimize other types of data. It's going to emphasize the people who can help you and minimize the people who don't want to help you. It's going to simultaneously emphasize the areas you need to grow to accomplish your vision as well as emphasize the belief that you can grow. It will minimize or delete beliefs you carry around about yourself that say you can't grow. It will emphasize paths more likely to help you create your future and minimize or delete all the paths you could take to other futures that you don't want. And most importantly, it will invite you to ask a different set of questions. Questions like:

How must I interpret my present life in order to best create my desired future?

What is the best interpretation of my past in order to make my preferred future the most likely to happen?

How must I see myself or my current coworkers or team or financial situation in order to set me up for future success?

What do I need to grab on to or value right now in order to pull myself into my desired future?

What people or values or beliefs do I need to let go of in order to create my desired future?

These are the questions that will begin to create "off-menu" realities for you. These are the questions that invite generative future thinking. You're not starting with what your current perspective *is*; you are starting with what perspective *must you choose* in order to create a future that would thrill you.

If this sounds confusing or overwhelming, never fear. Once you choose a future, your mind starts to filter for you, whether you like it or not. Just like when you buy a new (or old) car you start seeing it everywhere, and your mind starts to see paths to your future that it couldn't see before you got clear on which future you wanted to create. A lot of this happens automatically, just because you're connecting to a future that's reinterpreting your present for you.

One of my favorite stories about this is from one of my long-time clients, Jeff Lambert. Jeff is a serial entrepreneur. He's founded everything—from a top-fifty PR firm to a massively successful tech company to everything in between. To talk with Jeff is to brainstorm with him, and he is incredibly generous with his ideas. In fact, the subtitle of this book was inspired by a conversation with Jeff.

During one session, he mentioned to me that he was overwhelmed and might need a chief of staff.

"Might?" I said. "Do you need one or not?"

"I absolutely need one," he said.

"When would you like to have hired your new chief of staff?" I asked.

"It would be great to have them hired by the end of the year," he said (#defaultfuture).

It was July.

I asked, "How urgent is getting this position staffed?"

"It's my number-one priority."

"Okay," I said, "when would you love to have hired your new chief of staff? What would thrill you?"

He smiled. "I'd love to have my chief of staff hired in the next six weeks" (#generativefuture).

→ "Once you get a picture of the future that excites you, now you can leverage that future as a filter to begin interpreting the present."

His vision just shifted from six month to six weeks. At the time, he didn't really know how he was going to do it. But once we moved the goalposts up to six weeks, his mind was able to give it the urgency that his words were saying he felt. Suddenly, he started making requests of people he hadn't made before. He put the word out about what he was looking for to new people. He thought of people for the position who he hadn't really thought of before. When he was in meetings or at conferences or at parties, every person was a potential connection to him hiring a chief of staff. When someone showed interest, he didn't move slowly and let other tasks or priorities displace his focus. He followed up immediately. His filter from the future changed how he saw the present. Nights out became networking events. Every acquaintance became an opportunity. Even an opposing mediator who he met in litigation *against* him became a potential chief of staff.

Seriously.

The guy who ultimately became his chief of staff was the hired-gun negotiator working against him on a contentious dispute on behalf of a company Jeff had invested in. Despite frustrating and fruitless negotiations with the owner, Jeff was impressed by the MBA-touting and highly perceptive negotiator sitting across the table. So Jeff asked him, "I'm looking for a unique chief of staff role. Do you know anyone?" And six weeks later, Jeff hired him.

Six months ahead of his default future.

That's the power of vision. Vision turns adversaries into advocates. Vision transforms the messy present into the raw materials needed to mold an extraordinary future.

Not only that but imagine how much more Jeff was able to create simply by utilizing the power of vision. Think about how much work a person does in six months. Think about the value his new chief of staff brought to him and his organization in those six months. The progress they brought to Jeff and the team and Jeff's other projects. Think of the compounding effects his chief of staff brought him in the years since as friends and professional colleagues. All that would not have happened had he not gotten clear on what a vision for his future was that would actually thrill him.

It's not rocket science. It's simply the power of vision. It's the power of creating *from* the future.

LEVERAGING THE VISION OF TEAMS: GOING BEYOND YOUR PERSONAL VISION

But this tool isn't just about you. It affects others as well. When Jeff and I first started working together years ago, he looked at me and said, "I want to be the best client you've ever had." People don't usually talk (or think) like that. But I want to tell you: It feels great when someone says that to you. It's bold. It's a gift to you. It makes you want to become worthy of that kind of gift.

So I reflexively said back, "And I want to be the best coach you'll ever have." I instantly knew it was going to be a blast working together, and it has been. And it started with him casting a vision for himself to be my best client.

In that moment, he had created a visional environment. He and I created a culture of vision. He declared his desire to explore what he was capable of as a client, and that drew out my desire to explore what I was capable of as a coach. He elevated his vision, and that in turn elevated mine. In that moment, we became a meta-performing team.

You see, creating a future that excites you isn't just about having a personal vision. A person with the mindset of a meta performer participates in the collective cocreation of a team vision. At the firm and institute, we have a collective vision of creating a noble future (more on this in the last chapter). It's not something any of us can accomplish on our own. It's something we can only build together.

People who hire us know they have a next level inside

themselves, but they have difficulty accessing it. No one gets to the next level by themselves. So how do we help others get there? By unleashing their power to create visional teams and cultures.

A leader's job is to manage that tension of unleashing a vision of individuals and then tying those visions together, like disparate rocket ships coming together to synergistically launch them into the stratosphere. This is what Elon Musk is doing at SpaceX. When he's not busy trying to buy social media platforms, Elon is designing the most powerful rockets on earth in order to make humans a multiplanetary species. The kind of rockets that NASA used for fifty years were essentially six giant rockets to get the space shuttle into outer space. That was the best understanding of rockets at the time, but they were big and clumsy and had little control when it came to maneuvering. The engineers at SpaceX came up with a different solution: the Falcon Heavy has twenty-seven individual rockets that work in concert with each other. It's like witnessing art to watch those rockets work together to launch and navigate Falcon Heavy back to earth, each one working independently but in tandem with all the other rockets. Together they create nearly a million tons of pressure per square inch. It's pretty magical. When you have a collective of visionaries working together for a common goal, and you're all aligned, you can go farther than anyone ever imagined possible.

Meta performers don't just have visions that excite them. They have visions that have the power to align others with them. Together they can go places. How is this different from a high performer? High performers tend to think of every other rocket as competition. They tend to be vision narcissists. They are unidoxical thinkers. It's my vision against everyone else's. By contrast, a meta performer asks: *How can I help everyone on my team expand their vision?* Then how can I use those expanded visions to take us and others

→ "Meta performers ask: How can I help everyone on my team expand their vision?"

into the stratosphere together? So it moves the questions we're asking from "What's my vision? What excites me?" to "What's our vision? What excites us?"

So how do we do this? How do we expand our vision? The answer is growth.

 Want to go deeper on this topic? We've developed free resources for you and your team for each chapter, including discussion questions, recorded interviews with our coaches, and more. To access, scan the QR code or go to www.novus.global/book/chapter5.

CHAPTER 6

EXPANDING WHAT'S POSSIBLE

It's unbelievable how much you don't know about a game you've been playing your whole life.

———————————————→ MICKEY MANTLE

How Pistols Learn—Getting Wrong—Worse Than Faux Leather—
Writing One Hundred Books—Was Picasso Good Enough? —
Welcome to Seb's— Asymmetrical Risk and Running for President

The 1991 movie *The Pistol*, which is based on the life of NCAA basketball legend Pete "Pistol" Maravich,[1] tells of how his visionary father and basketball coach, Press Maravich, helped to transform the game of basketball. One of my favorite scenes in that movie is when Press addresses his team at practice. He says, "I am not spending valuable hours of my life just to teach you boys to throw a ball through an iron hoop. This is a way of life. I want players to think, work, sweat, challenge themselves, discipline themselves, because anything else just isn't worth it, to anyone." Then he pauses and says with compassion, "The problem with you boys is simple. You're all a bunch of dummies 'cause you think you know it all."

This might sound harsh, but it is the biggest challenge all high performers face. After all, isn't it what we know that makes us a high performer? But meta performers flip this on its head: it's what we think we know that makes us ignorant. In the film, Coach Maravich proceeds to grab a ball from one of his players and draws a small circle on it, and says, "You see this circle? The size of this circle represents everything that I know about basketball." Then he holds the ball out and says, "But the size of this ball represents everything about the game that has never been discovered." Then he puts a tiny dot on the ball, and says, "This dot is what you all know, combined." [2]

I think about that scene every day. Some days I relive that scene as Coach Maravich talking to his players. On my best days, I relive it as one of his players. Every time we hire anyone at the firm or institute, we draw the same circle. When I hired my chief of staff, I drew a big circle and said, "This circle represents everything there is to know in the universe about being a world-class chief of staff." Then I drew a much smaller circle: "This is how much you know." And then I drew a dot: "That's how much I know." There are two important points to this: The candidate knows more than I do—that's partly why we're hiring them—but neither of us know what's possible in that role. They weren't hired just for the small circle of what they know, and they weren't just hired because they know more than me. They were hired *to explore how big they can get their circle of competence to be.*

Think about what you're good at. Maybe it's leadership or finances or politics or public speaking or a particular sport or running a nonprofit or being a parent. How large would you draw the circle that shows how much you know about what you're good at? And how much bigger is the circle that represents *how much there is to know* about what you're good at? The closer those circles are to the same size, the more probable it is that you're living from a high-performance mindset and not a meta-performing mindset. There's more potential to explore than you realize.

And this is great news.

It's great news because if you already know most of what there is to know, then the most rewarding part of your life is behind you.

This capacity for growth is represented by the Buddhist idea of "Shoshin," or what some call "A Beginner's Mind," or what Jeff Bezos calls "Day 1,"[3] where he constantly reminds his team to act as if they're starting over and to be inspired by all the potential success in front of them rather than resting on all the success that is behind them. Interestingly, at Amazon, they say they look for leaders "who are right, a lot."[4] Yet they also say that "leaders work to disconfirm their beliefs." This is a paradox I don't want you to move past: Leaders are right a lot but also work to disconfirm their beliefs. High performers are usually great at the first part and horrible at the second. This is because typical high performers usually think, *If my beliefs are right, why would I seek to disconfirm them?* But meta performers understand that in order to be right a lot you have to seek out where you might be wrong. In other words, what people think they're right about today is what's keeping them from being right tomorrow. This illustrates a very important part of growth that people forget: in order to grow, you've got to get wrong.

ON BEING WRONG

Think about a time you were wrong. It's actually challenging for most of us to think about a time we were wrong because our minds are designed to learn from mistakes but not necessarily remember them. As Kathryn Schulz wrote about brilliantly in her book *Being Wrong: Adventures in the Margin of Error* we're simply not wired to store memories of being wrong on a daily basis; we're much more wired to correct mistakes and then act as if that's what we believed all along.[5] But most of us, if we try really hard, can remember a time when we've been wrong about something or someone. Maybe it was a bad hire or a bad date or when we made a wrong turn or ordered the wrong thing on Amazon or ordered the right thing but sent it to the wrong address. Whether you can remember a time or not, let me ask you a question:

What does it feel like being wrong?

When our coaches ask this to a room full of people, invariably people will shout out: embarrassing, frustrating, humiliating. But that's *not* what it feels like to be wrong. Then we walk them through Kathryn Schulz's work, which taught us that embarrassment and frustration and humiliation are what we experience *once we discover we're wrong.* But how does it feel to be wrong *before we realize we're wrong?*

It feels *exactly like being right.*

Being wrong and being right feel exactly the same up until the moment we discover we're wrong. This is one of the most important ideas for high performers to remember as they reflect on their life and the next level of growth for them. Your greatest opportunities for growth are hiding behind what you're certain you're right about. One time I was working with an incredibly gifted high performer, and after a few sessions of her being right about everything, I finally said, "The object of the game here is for us to get wrong together. Your growth is limited so long as you keep thinking you're right."

I usually ask what it feels like to be wrong to get people curious about what they think they don't know. During our trainings, we teach companies the wisdom of Epictetus: that the hardest thing to learn is that which we think we already know. Or to quote Mark Twain: "It ain't what you don't know that gets you into trouble. It's what you know for sure that just ain't so." This is never truer than when it comes to growth.

There are so many people right now who honestly believe they are "growing" or that they have adopted the "growth mindset." But in the words of physicist Richard

→ "How does it feel to be wrong before we realize we're wrong? It feels exactly like being right."

Feynman, "The first principle is that you must not fool yourself, but the easiest person to fool is you." Most people think they have a growth mindset, but from our experience what they actually have is a false growth mindset.

FALSE GROWTH MINDSET

World-renowned Stanford University psychologist Dr. Carol Dweck argued in her book *Mindset: The New Psychology of Success* that a person's mindset was the definitive factor in one's success. She broke down the types of mindsets into either fixed or growth mindsets. Most of us are familiar with this concept. People with fixed mindsets believe their abilities and skills are "fixed," and those who adopt a growth mindset believe their abilities can be developed. After the broad acceptance of her ideas and book, however, she realized a phenomenon had taken place. She determined that far too many people oversimplified her findings, which led to having a "false growth mindset." In an interview with *The Atlantic*, she described the false growth mindset as:

> Saying you have growth mindset when you don't really have it or you don't really understand [what it is]. It's also false in the sense that nobody has a growth mindset in everything all the time. Everyone is a mixture of fixed and growth mindsets. You could have a predominant growth mindset in an area but there can still be things that trigger you into a fixed mindset trait. Something really challenging and outside your comfort zone can trigger it, or, if you encounter someone who is much better than you at something you pride yourself on, you can think "Oh, that person has ability, not me." So I think we all, students and adults, have to look for our fixed-mindset triggers and understand when we are falling into that mindset. I think a lot of what happened [with false growth mindset among educators] is that instead of taking this long and difficult journey, where you work

on understanding your triggers, working with them, and over time being able to stay in a growth mindset more and more, many educators just said, "Oh yeah, I have a growth mindset" because either they know it's the right mindset to have or they understood it in a way that made it seem easy.[6]

With a false growth mindset, it looks like you have a growth mindset, but you don't. Just like faux leather, it kind of looks like the real thing, but it isn't. In our firm, to protect against a false growth mindset, everyone is always getting coached. To put this another way: everyone in our company is on a performance improvement plan from the day they're hired to the day they leave. We have veteran coaches, and we have new coaches. Everyone in the firm is always getting coached by somebody. We mix everybody up so that at any moment one of our most veteran coaches might be getting coached by one of our newest coaches. This approach challenges the false notion that new people have nothing to offer veteran or experienced coaches. When we first started this, we'd have coaches ask, "What do I have to learn from someone who is not as 'good' as me?" When that happened, we knew we were working with a false growth mindset. In contrast, I always enjoy picking the newest coaches to coach me, and I almost always get the best results. Regardless of the coach's "experience," I'm committed to creating value. I am not relying on them for my growth. I am relying on them to facilitate growth. This happens sometimes with potential clients. When one of our coaches was talking to someone looking for a coach, they asked our coach, "Have you ever run a company with fifty million dollars in revenue?"

Our coach answered honestly and said, "No."

The client said, "Then why would I hire you? You've never done what I've done." The irony of this story is that the client was talking to a coach who was currently coaching another executive who was running a company worth $100 million, and that client was getting immense value from the coaching. But the potential client falsely believed, "If you've never done it, you have nothing for me." Oftentimes opportunities to grow are hiding where we believe they can't be. We're blinded by our beliefs about where growth comes from. One of the hallmarks of a false growth mindset is the notion that a person can only grow in the right environment, under the perfect conditions, or with the "right person."

FALSE GROWTH MINDSET	META PERFORMANCE MINDSET
Focused on past growth.	Focused on present and future growth.
Based on feelings. *"I feel like I'm growing."*	Based on results. *"Proof of growing."*
Haphazard about growth. Has no plan.	Has a plan for growth.
Gets defensive when invited to grow.	Gets excited when invited to grow.
Looking for ways they have grown.	Looking for new ways to grow.
I've reached the summit.	There is no summit.

Another hallmark of the false growth mindset is how they measure growth. If you ask someone, "How do you know you have a growth mindset?" They will almost always all look to the past.

"I've grown so much! My family has grown. My company has grown. So, obviously, I have a growth mindset." But true growth doesn't use the past as a measurement. In the first place, some things grow by accident, with or without you. This is called "momentum," and it's amazing, but it isn't the same thing as having a growth mindset. No, a growth mindset doesn't look to the past but to the present and future. Meta performers want to grow and can answer the question, "Where are you currently attempting to grow?" They don't let past growth seduce them into ignoring their future potential.

LEANING INTO GROWTH

Whenever I'm looking to hire a coach for myself to help me grow, I look for someone who can out-dream me. Put another way: I'm looking for coaches and mentors who see more capacity for growth in me than I see in myself. To me, one of the worst things you can ever be is a coach who is intimidated by or satisfied with your client's dreams for themselves. That's why when we work with clients, after we get clear on a vision that would excite them, we invite them to think about an *even bigger dream*. Not because they *should* go after a bigger dream (that's up to them). But just to see what happens when they're invited into one.

Here's a recent example: While writing this book, our firm hired Mary Curran-Hackett to help us get these ideas onto paper. Mary is a world-class writer and has helped many leaders turn their ideas into bestselling books. But I didn't just want her to capture our ideas on paper. I wanted her to experience what it was we do with the clients we serve. So one day during a writing session I offered for her to work with one of our top coaches, Deb Foy, for three months so she could get a taste of what we do. During that time with Deb, she got clear on her vision, which was to write five books a year. Now, that may seem impossible to someone who has never drafted a book, but for Mary that's just another year at the office. Since Mary knew this was what she was already planning to do, Deb asked her about how she felt about expanding that goal. How about writing twenty or even one hundred books? Deb was inviting her to grow her vision.

These questions were revealing for Mary because they got her to consider the gaps between her current reality and the vision Deb just proposed. At first one hundred books sounded not only impossible but undesirable. Writing one hundred books the way she was currently doing it sounded like a kind of indentured servitude. The idea initially prompted a prisoner-mindset response. But after exploring all her objections, Mary and Deb discovered a way she could "write" one hundred books a year or more. She could create a Mastermind course where she mentored hundreds, if not thousands, of aspiring writers to finally get their ideas onto paper. She began moving toward that plan, and before we were done writing this book she had already created a pilot program, and she was on her way to helping more people write books than she ever thought possible.

She didn't know she could do that.

So, as we invite clients to grow their vision, we realize that these long-held and unconscious beliefs start to bubble up to the surface. These beliefs are there whether we realize it or not, *but they only surface when we try to grow*. That's why we challenge our clients to think about what they perceive is holding them back. As they list their limitations or excuses, we may counter them with: "Is that really true?" This usually gets them to start digging a little deeper. Here we are able to start testing and exploring with them what is *truly* holding them back. This vision-growth conversation tills the soil. We're able to get in there and see what's actually going on beneath the surface.

When meeting with clients, we pose the question about their vision this way: "Imagine if we worked together for a year, and it was just wildly successful. Imagine you had the kind of success that makes you fall to your knees in gratitude. What would we need to do together in order for you to have that experience?"

This is where we begin to have fun. Because it gives people the permission to imagine, to dream, to go window-shopping for the future. When we're in this phase, we're not committing to any specific goal. One of the critical challenges for most high performers is they think, *I've set a goal; now I have to achieve it.* Most high performers are executors. They feel like there's no space for them to talk aloud without anything being at stake. When we're coaching, we create a safe space for them to just go on a stroll and date multiple futures through conversation. Then we start listening for what lights them up and resonates with them. We may even ask them one of the best questions you can ask someone, which we've already mentioned: *What would be worth suffering for?*

The difference between a good coach and a great coach is a good coach will ask, "What do you want?" and then help you get it. A *great* coach will listen to what would thrill you *and turn that into a baseline*—not your top line. Once we get clear on what would be great for you, that's where the real fun starts. This is where we get to play. Because when we coach like this, we may find out that the writer writing five books a year doesn't want to write twenty or one hundred. She wants to help write thousands, or even millions of books. So our task would be: How can we help her do that?

A good coach is looking for the resistance, excuses, and stories you're telling yourself and then problem-solving for those. But a great coach is actively creating resistance. It's like what a great physical trainer does. For example, a friend of mine lost a lot of weight and has been working with a physical trainer. I asked her why she loved her trainer so much. And her answer was, "She always gives me more than I think I can handle." Likewise, a great coach will help you explore a bigger vision than you think you can handle. A great coach will invite you to test your limits, explore your appetite to dream, and expand your own belief in what you are capable of doing. It will need a lot of resistance training, challenges, failures, and a complete overhaul of one's life. It's also going to require a team to make it possible.

Here is a little-known fact about most high performers that even they don't realize is true: they are typically operating from a very limited vision for their future. It doesn't seem limited to *them*. And it especially doesn't seem limited to those around them. But it's limited all the same. This is because most high performers have their heads down, hustling, trying to "win" but rarely lifting their heads out of the trench they're in to ask, "Am I winning at what I want to win at?" or "Is there a better way to do this?" And it's limited by the question, *Where can I be the best?* Since high performers are motivated by success, they tend to pick visions where they will be guaranteed the feeling of satisfaction or a perceived "win." Meta performers, as we now know, ask *What am I capable of?* This question itself implies it's not something they currently see or are aware exists—it lies beyond their current field of vision. Vision casting for meta performers requires looking beyond anything they think is now possible. Even if it means they might fail. And since most high performers hate to fail, they rarely set their sights on something they may struggle to or never attain at all. In sum, their fear of failure diminishes the visions they allow themselves to have.

Many high performers wouldn't admit this though. Years ago I asked a leader: "What are you doing to improve our capacity for vision casting?" He said to me, "I'm already good enough at that." Let me tell you something: I've never met a leader who is "good enough" at vision casting. It's truly one of the hardest things to do, and it is an endless art. As a leader, saying you're already good enough at vision casting is like Picasso saying he's already good enough at painting or that Mother Teresa is already good enough at serving the poor. Is it true? Maybe. Was Picasso or Mother Teresa interested in "good enough"? Hardly. So the question isn't "how good are you at vision casting" but "how good are you capable of becoming?"

WILLINGNESS TO MAKE MISTAKES AND INTENTIONAL GROWTH

One major component to growth requires experimentation. Growth demands that we try new things. That we risk failure. That we do things that may not work out the way that we plan so that we can learn and iterate.

For example, I am relearning to play the piano. My parents paid for lessons when I was a kid from a great teacher (here's to you, Melissa Sturdivan). But then I got into high school and college, and I picked up the guitar instead (guitars travel better than pianos do).

Fast-forward twenty years, and a global pandemic happened. I found myself shut in and alone in my home for months. Most of our work at the firm and institute was remote, so that didn't change much. But what did change was when work was over, I had essentially Netflix and worrying about toilet paper to keep me company. Instead of staying home, I would get in my car and drive up the Pacific Coast Highway, but then they shut down the roads with military vehicles due to people trying to destroy storefronts in Santa Monica.

I needed a hobby.

I did puzzles for a while, but to be honest those kind of stressed me out (*winstophobia* is the "fear of jigsaw puzzles." Just FYI).

So after a while I bought a cheap piano synthesizer, put it on my dining-room table, and started to practice every day.

Years later, I still play nearly every day. And I gotta say, I'm getting pretty good.[7]

Of course, learning (or relearning) something new can be difficult. I find that with the piano I get into a "performance rut." There are certain songs I know how to play ("God Only Knows" by Brian Wilson and "Maybe I'm Amazed" by Paul McCartney, for example). And being in a rut gets, by definition, kind of old. This is the paradox of performance. Being good at something isn't all it's cracked up to be. Getting better at something is where it's at. So I asked myself: "Do I just want to play the same songs over and over again that I'm good at or do I want to step into the pain, the awkwardness, and sometimes the shame of not being very good and learn something new?" A young banjo prodigy was once asked how he was able to become so advanced so soon, and he answered, "Every day I do something I don't know." The high performer is going to resist doing something new or something they don't know. They will resist looking stupid or awkward.

Perfection is their game. A meta performer wants to keep pushing the boundaries of what they know and are capable of, even if it means they will fumble. You won't ever get better at playing the same music. You need to intentionally step into areas that will force you to grow.

With the piano, I wanted to get better. So I flip-turned from easier rock hits and moved to film scores. I had always loved the film *La La Land* starring Emma Stone and Ryan Gosling. I love jazz, and I adore the music in the film by Justin Hurwitz. So I bought the sheet music to that amazing piece "Mia's Theme," where Ryan Gosling goes full-tilt jazz when all J. K. Simmons wants is for him to play Christmas music. I love that scene. I practiced that piece for over six months, and I got okay at it. But then I hit another performance wall. I just couldn't get my fingers to move as fast as Ryan's do in the film. That could have been the end, but then I thought, *I wonder who taught Ryan how to play like that*. After some internet sleuthing, I found the person who was Ryan's personal musical trainer for the film and reached out to them and had an amazing conversation. I could have reached out to probably anyone, but if you're going to learn how to play like Sebastian from *La La Land* , who better than to talk to the person who taught Sebastian in *La La Land*.

Fast-forward another year, I found myself in the Miami Airport sky lounge playing the piano there in public for the first time in my life.

I got tipped five dollars.

I wasn't particularly good. But if you would have told me five years ago that I'd be playing jazz in a piano bar in Miami for tips, I would have told you that was impossible.

I didn't know I could do that.

Of course, playing the piano isn't core to my business (thank God). And so I take risks to grow within my work as well. I hire various coaches to coach me and go to coaching trainings to pick up new skills and try new experiments with my clients. I even have clients who I've been working with for years who say, "I'll be your guinea pig. Try any new stuff on me." The same is true in my leadership. I'm constantly looking for new ways to upgrade my leadership from books, blogs, podcasts, mentors, conferences, and coaches. Our team is constantly experimenting with various ways to lead meetings, structure the business, make things fun, and maximize our collective potential. Sometimes they work; sometimes they don't work. But we know part of being in our culture is that we're all guinea pigs, including me. At the end of the year, I make it a point to write down every failure we had to remind myself that we failed and are still breathing, and also so that I can remember to keep taking risks and keep iterating in the next year.

People who are unwilling to be bad, who don't move out of their comfort zone or do anything new, never discover what they're capable of. The reality is, there are no shortcuts to growth, only first steps. If you want to know what it's like to skydive, you have to jump out of the plane. If you want to produce or direct a film, you have to produce and direct a film. If you want to play the piano, you're going to have to play the piano. The first few (or many) times are

→ "People who are unwilling to be bad, who don't move out of their comfort zones or do anything new, never discover what they're capable of."

going to be "bad." Everything you do right out of the gate isn't going to be incredible, but you will learn more from those mistakes and failures than not doing it all.

DESIGNING YOUR LIFE FOR ASYMMETRIC RISK

You want to get really good at learning the difference between failures that are formative and failures that are fatal, and you want to obviously stay away from the fatal failures and you want to really lean into the formative ones. As *New York Times* bestselling author Ray Dalio says, "I believe that the key to success lies in knowing how to both strive for a lot and fail well. By failing well, I mean being able to experience painful failures that provide big learnings without failing badly enough to get knocked out of the game."[8]

Fools either don't ever try to fail or fail in ways that are fatal. In other words, you need to get comfortable designing risks that will make you grow—not kill you. These are sometimes called "asymmetrical risks." Technically, an asymmetrical risk is one in which there is potential for a big upside with little downside. But there's a kind of risk that's even better than that. My favorite asymmetrical risks are those that even if you lose, you win. It's not just that there's a small downside; *there is no downside.* There's only upside. These types of risks don't usually exist naturally. They have to be designed. For example, most people don't realize this, but running for president of the United States is an asymmetrical risk. Even if you lose, for the rest of your life, every time you're introduced anywhere you are a "mom, attorney . . . and former candidate for president of the United States." The amount of benefits people get from running for any kind of office (brand recognition, relationships, prominence in a political party, etc.) often far outweigh the cost of losing an election if the campaigns are designed well.

You see, there are some things that aren't worth doing even if you're successful. Then there are other things that are worth doing *only* if you're successful. That's where most people live. If they take risks at all, they take risks that "had better work."

But then there are meta performers.

Meta performers take risks that are worth doing whether they're successful or not. In *The Pistol*, Press Maravich finishes his pep talk by saying, "Now if you'll forget about the girls and cars and listen to me, you can accomplish things that you never thought were possible. I don't care if you're short, slow, tall, or small. You can play with the best of them if you'll dedicate yourself to becoming better." It bears repeating: *You'll accomplish the thing you never thought possible . . . if you'll dedicate yourself to becoming better.* In business and on teams, you want to be intentionally creating opportunities for growth as much as possible.

Because until you do, you're still in prison.

Keep reading to find out why.

 Want to go deeper on this topic? We've developed free resources for you and your team for each chapter, including discussion questions, recorded interviews with our coaches, and more. To access, scan the QR code or go to www.novus.global/book/chapter6.

CHAPTER 7
ESCAPING INVISIBLE CAGES

It wasn't me.

→ SHAGGY

Why the Best Entrepreneurs Are in Jail—Gag Reflexes—Intuitive Fences—Saving Forty Dollars Searching for Agency—Hypnotic Blame—Watch Your Mouth—Being on the Hook—Herbie Hancock's Greatest Mistake

I remember the first time I went to prison.

The clang of a two-ton metal door shutting behind me and the muted electric buzz of a lock switching into place reminded me that I had just entered a very difficult place to escape from. A group of high-performing leaders in business from the outside had been invited to spend the day with inmates who had volunteered to be part of a program called CEO of Your Own Life, designed to help them refocus their entrepreneurial abilities toward endeavors that get them a job rather than arrested. In the words of Greg Boyle, Jesuit priest and founder of Homeboy Industries in Los Angeles, "Nothing stops a bullet like a job." And this program was meant to help them do just that upon release.

As we walked through several gated security checkpoints, I was told the men we were going to visit were more nervous to meet us than we were to meet them. With my palms sweating and my heart pounding, I found that hard to believe. But after spending a day with the men inside, I realized they were right. We learned firsthand that the guys inside were humbly surprised that anyone would choose to come and visit them. Some of them hadn't had visitors in years. Many of their family and friends had—sometimes understandably—disowned them. So for complete strangers to sacrifice a day to invest in them filled them with gratitude.

What started as a one-day visit turned into years of serving on the board with the organization that allowed us to be there: Defy Ventures, a nonprofit dedicated to reducing recidivism rates in prisons and giving people a second chance. Many of our coaches and faculty at the institute have since donated and participated on regional boards of Defy Ventures, as well as coached several of their leaders nationwide, along with volunteering with both the incarcerated and those who have been released.

Put simply: Defy Ventures programs *work*. When prisoners (Defy calls them EIT's, "entrepreneurs in training") go through their programs, their likelihood of returning to prison drops, and their probability of employment goes up. The nationwide recidivism rate for people released from prison is over 45 percent. That means nearly half of all people let out of prison will one day return. Astonishingly, the recidivism rate for Defy graduates is less than 10 percent. One of Defy's key objectives to ensure prisoners don't return is to help them develop not only the skill sets they'll need out in the workforce but the mindset to stay out of prison once they are released.

And that includes developing what meta performers call an "ownership mindset."

Over the years, I've talked to many people who have spent hard time in jail and listened to them share about the forces at play that lure a person back into prison. As you can imagine, prison is a place that is rife with blame. As it's said in one of my favorite movies: "Everyone's innocent in Shawshank." The same is true in just about every prison I've visited. And as you get to know their individual stories, it's easy to see all the opportunities for blame. After all, many of them came from tough backgrounds. In prison, I met a man who got into a fight when he was *eight years old*—no one was hurt, and the story reminded me of several scuffles my older sister and I got into when we were in elementary school—but instead of a slap on the wrist and maybe a scolding from Mom and Dad, he was sent to juvenile hall. This jump-starts what sociologists call the "school-to-prison pipeline," the phenomenon of certain kids from certain neighborhoods being unintentionally, though predictably, guided into the prison system.

The reality is, most of these children never get a first chance, let alone the second chance that, as adults, Defy Ventures is offering them. If you're going to sympathize with anybody blaming the system, blaming schools, blaming police, blaming gangs, blaming their family, you can sympathize with many of these men and women.

Yet while there's plenty of blame to go around, and the blame is often appropriate, it is almost never helpful. This is a hard distinction for most of us to make. While all truth is true, not all truth is helpful. While a fact may make us feel better, not all facts are useful for helping us improve our lives. This is the great seduction of blame: it lures us into truths that don't help us advance in our lives while ignoring the truths that will. The more we give ourselves to blame, the less agency we begin to experience in our lives.

One of my mentors who helped design the original curriculum for Defy's programs and had spent decades working with incarcerated men and women once told me, "You want to know when I know someone isn't going back to prison?"

"When's that?" I asked.

"When you see them own their role in being there in the first place."

If you deeply care about someone and the trajectory of their life, you'll care about the amount of responsibility they're bringing to their life. If you care about others, you'll care about their ownership.

The same is even more true when it comes to caring about yourself.

As strange as it may sound, high performers struggle with blame just like everyone else. Blame is no respecter of previous performance. One of my favorite films, *The Usual Suspects*, has one of the best quotes, spoken by the narrator of the film named Verbal Kint. He says, "The greatest trick the devil ever pulled is convincing the world he doesn't exist."

The same is true with blame. It loves to convince you it isn't there.

Yet no matter who you are—whether you're the most successful person you know or the smartest person in most rooms you're in, or whatever metric you use to evaluate your own life—blame is there, sneaking around, poking holes in the balloon of your life, stealing your agency, diminishing your will, and draining you of the energy you need to create the life you were meant to live.

The question isn't whether blame is diminishing your life or not; it's *where*.

→ "If you deeply care about someone and the trajectory of their life, you'll care about the amount of responsibility they're bringing to their life. If you care about others, you'll care about their ownership."

HOW TO FIND HIDING BLAME

When I was a kid, the school nurse would come to our class and teach us how to floss. She would give us these red tablets to chew to show if we had plaque on our teeth. The red tablets stuck to the plaque so you could see with the naked eye all the plaque you were missing by not flossing. It was awesome. I remember looking at Laura Miley sitting next to me after she chewed the red tablet.

She was smiling, and her teeth were red all over the place. I started to laugh at her. Then I suddenly realized she was laughing at me. Unbeknown to me, my teeth were even more red than hers. We all laughed at each other until we realized we all had the same problem.[1] When it comes to blame, we're all walking around with proverbial plaque on our teeth and laughing at everyone else for blaming others. We simply can't see where we're doing it too. We need the help of a little red tablet.

Our favorite red tablet in coaching is a concept called your "intuitive fence." Imagine there was a barrier or fence around your life created by your intuition of what you believed was possible or impossible for your future. Things that fall inside the fence, we feel are "possible" for us. Things that fall outside the fence are things we deem as "impossible" for us. Generally, if our intuition tells us something is impossible, we tend to listen to it. If it tells us something is possible, we tend to believe that too. So, if our intuition tells us we can't make $10 million next year—or $100 million or $100 billion or whatever—we tend to behave as if that were true. If our intuition tells us we *can* make $10 million next year, we tend to behave as if that were true. Yet while our intuition does its best to tell us the truth about the world, Nobel Prize–winning economist Daniel Kahneman believes that our intuition often fails to tell us what is true, especially about the future.[2] Kahneman argues that we can trust our intuition when it's been *well trained* in specific, often linear settings. But in a dynamic, mostly nonlinear world, training our intuitions is difficult, which means our intuitions are often . . . off. This doesn't mean we ignore our intuition; it just means we don't blindly trust it. Rather than naively trusting our intuition, we test it. And the more we test our intuition, the more we can trust it.

The intuitive fence is a tool to do just that.

Here's how it works: The closer to the center of your fence you are, the more possible things occur to you. So making $1,000 in the next year of your life probably occurs to you as very possible. But as that number grows, it gets closer and closer to the edge of the fence, until it crosses a threshold of "possible but not probable" to "not possible."

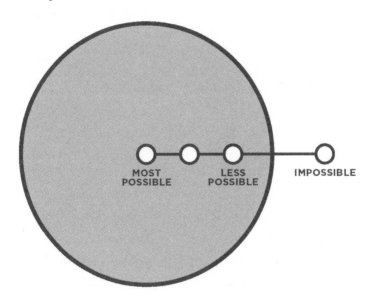

MOST POSSIBLE   LESS POSSIBLE   IMPOSSIBLE

One interesting caveat to the intuitive fence is that some people, especially high performers, don't like to admit that things are not possible for them. They've trained themselves to believe that "anything is possible." This is certainly better than training ourselves that most things are impossible for us. Yet everyone has things they believe are not possible for them. So high performers' standard way of dealing with things they don't believe are possible is to not think about those things at all. For example, I am currently making no plans to make $10 trillion. The idea of even trying to do that seems ridiculous to me. I don't even think about it. That's because things I believe to be impossible become invisible to me. In turn, this means you can know what you think is impossible for yourself based not on what you say you believe but on what you're willing to try to accomplish.

While I'm using money as an example, you could also use productivity of a team or fulfillment in a relationship or the size of your impact in the world or the success of a piece of art you create. We have intuitive fences for all those things. There are things we believe are possible in our relationships and things we believe are impossible. There are things we believe are possible for any of our creative endeavors and things we believe are impossible. No matter what we're talking about, there are completely possible futures for you that are invisible to you simply because your intuition has told you, often without you knowing, that those things are impossible for you.

So whenever we start working with our coaching clients, we teach them about Intuitive Fences and then invite them to expand them and see what happens. As an example (to go back to money), let's say someone wants to make X amount of money in the next year. We might ask, "Why not double that?" or "Why not ten times that?" The point of asking the question isn't because $2X$ or $10X$ of what they originally said was better. They can pick whatever amount they want. We're not primarily concerned about what the number is. But we keep inviting them beyond their intuitive fence until it triggers what we might call the *blame reflex*. This is similar to a gag reflex—in which our throat and stomach spontaneously respond when they feel like they're in danger. Gagging, as unpleasant and unbecoming as it is, isn't bad; it protects us. In the same way, our minds have a spontaneous blame reflex whenever our sense of identity is in danger. This identity can be threatened when someone criticizes us ("You're a loser!"). But it can also be threatened when someone invites us into more ("You could change the world!"). A blame reflex is when we spontaneously, unconsciously start creating defenses for our limitations when pushed to our perceived capacity. It's what we noticed with Mary in the previous chapter when Deb invited her to consider how she might write one hundred books in a year. The blame reflex sounds a lot like:

That would never work.

That can't happen.

He/she/they would never go for it.

That's impossible.

That's never been done before.

Someone is already doing it.

I don't have time for that.

We can't do that, because my spouse would hate it.

We can't do that, because my kids would never go for it.

The market doesn't want it.

Other people with more resources and power have already taken up that space.

Good coaches intentionally trigger that blame reflex to hunt for areas in our lives where we have abdicated our responsibility and that we may not be aware of. So long as these beliefs run around unexamined, our lives remain trapped by blame. But if we can spook them out into the open air, like a hunting dog forcing birds into flight, then we can examine them and decide if we want to keep them or leave them behind. This point cannot be overemphasized: the purpose of flushing out our beliefs, of taking the red tablet, of stimulating the blame reflex, is not to judge the beliefs. They may very well be helpful beliefs that we want to keep around. We simply won't know until we get them out and then play with them.

The intuitive fence conversation and the subsequent litany of defenses that follow always shine a light where you may be abdicating your responsibility. It exposes things you can't see on your own. You have to look at where you're placing the blame. What are

→ "Good coaches intentionally trigger the blame reflex to hunt for areas in our lives where we have abdicated our responsibility that we may not be aware of."

the stories you're telling yourself? What are the excuses you continually fall back on as to why your life isn't working out for you as you would like it to?

How are you letting yourself off the hook?

ON THE HOOK

Have you ever wanted someone to "give you a break" or "cut you some slack" or "let you off the hook"? When I do large talks with people, I often ask the crowd, "Have you ever let someone off the hook?" Everyone raises their hand. Then I ask if they've ever wanted somebody to let them off the hook? When I don't want to be responsible for something, I want someone to let me off the hook. Most people talk about letting people off the hook as an act of compassion. "I'm going to let her off the hook." But where does all growth happen for a person? On the hook or off the hook?

When I let somebody off the hook, what I'm really saying is, "I don't care about your growth." If you're committed to creating a culture of ownership, then you're going to have to get comfortable inviting people, including yourself, to put themselves on the hook. You want to invite everyone who's involved not to ask the question, *Who should be taking responsibility for this?* Rather, they should ask, *How can I take responsibility for this?* Our teams are so passionate about this idea that one of our coaches has a tattoo on her arm of a hook because it reminds her to stay on it.

ON THE HOOK	OFF THE HOOK
Searching primarily for *my* role, contribution, or responsibility in the situation.	Searching primarily for *others'* roles, contribution, and responsibility in the situation.
Wanting to grow.	*Wanting* to cut some slack.
Makes *amends*.	Makes *excuses*.
Requests forgiveness.	*Avoids* acknowledging gaps.
Focus on improvement.	Focus on *feeling better*.
Consequences that help us grow.	*No consequences*, no growth.
"The buck stops here."	"It's their fault."

One of my favorite examples of a team coming together to put themselves on the hook is from Bill Foy, who used to be an executive at a $40 billion international automotive company. Just to put that in perspective, that means his company wasn't a Fortune 500 company but a Global 500 company—one of the largest companies in the world—based out of Japan.

"Our team had been given a challenge from our parent company to cut operating expenses. Usually, our response to such a request was to get defensive and to fight for our budget. But this time we tried something different. Instead of getting defensive," Bill said, "we leaned into vision."[3] Bill brought in coaches and trainers from our team to help facilitate sessions where they could dream together. What emerged was a vision for their team to become the "best in class" of any automotive company in the world. This vision was exciting to the team, and it also meant they had to learn how to cut cost while increasing quality. With that vision they had chosen for themselves, cutting costs now didn't feel like a mandate from on high but an opportunity to explore what they were capable of as leaders.

"We used the intuitive fence to do that," Bill said. "At first we set targets like 'cut cost 6 percent in three years,' and then someone else said, 'Well, what about *8 percent* in three years?'" But then Bill noticed something beginning to happen. "There was like a tipping point. As we kept increasing the number, people began to shift from defensive to creative. At around the 15 percent mark, they started to get really energized. They started to believe in themselves."

And then someone threw out a number that sounded completely absurd: cut costs 30 percent in three years. No one knew how to do that. It was way outside their intuitive fences.

As Bill told me in an interview with him, "What's interesting is that as we wrestled with what would excite us and even scare us a little, one by one the various teams started to own it. They started to take responsibility for this extreme goal for themselves. It became like a game. It was something that I had never experienced in the company before. It really brought the team together."

"That's something I learned from all this," Bill said. "When you set a really big goal, it creates an opportunity to really bring people together and to learn from each other."

What they began to notice was that as they kept expanding the goal, a common complaint kept coming up: "They'll never let us do that." This was the biggest excuse—the biggest limiting belief—that had kept them from trying new things for years. "That's not how they do it at our competitors," or "That's not how we've ever done it before." But through Bill's leadership and the coaching, instead of using that belief as a de facto reality to protect the status quo, they got curious about it. Was that *really* true? Was it true that "they" wouldn't let them innovate? After some exploration, they realized it wasn't true at all. And once they realized they had the freedom to try new things, in Bill's words, "That's when the creativity really started to flow."

I was personally coaching Bill at the time, and one of my favorite questions to ask him was, "If you could talk to anybody about how to solve these creative challenges, who would you talk to?" And so Bill would go out and talk to the most innovative companies he could find outside his industry to learn best practices that people in automotive had never tried before.

Eventually, they came up with a plan. But it wasn't a plan to cut 30 percent of costs. They came up with a strategy to *exceed* 30 percent. Over the next three years, they saved the company over *$40 million.*

That's what happens when you combine vision with growth and ownership.

WATCH YOUR MOUTH

Another tool for shifting our lives from off the hook to on the hook is to notice and change our language. Here's what I mean:

About one hundred years ago, a children's psychologist named Lev Vygotsky noticed that most children, well, talk to themselves. A lot. Ethan Kross writes in his book *Chatter: The Voice in Our Head, Why It Matters, and How to Harness It*: "Unlike other leading thinkers of the time who thought this behavior was a sign of unsophisticated development, Vygotsky saw language playing a critical role in *how we learn to control ourselves*" (emphasis added).[4]

Our future is determined by choices in the present, and our present choices (read: our control over ourselves) is determined in large part by the conversations we're having with ourselves. Lev observed a process as children listened to others talking to them (usually adults or authority figures), they'd mimic those conversations with themselves, then they'd develop their own "out loud" conversations, and then those conversations would shift from talking out loud to having the conversation entirely in their own minds, becoming invisible to those around them. As he looked at how children talked to themselves, he got a glimpse of how self-talk shaped a person's mind. After all, we are constantly talking to ourselves about nearly everything, and children talking to themselves out loud shows the origins of the internal dialogue we've been carrying around our whole lives—making observations and judgments and telling ourselves stories about why things are the way they are. When you start to take a closer look at those stories and excuses, you can examine the underlying beliefs behind them. Then you can start to test all the beliefs and stories out. The point of examining where you're placing blame is so when those stories come up, you can test them. You can find out which ones are actually true and valid. You can examine them rather than having them serving as a kind of virus in your operating system, messing with your programming, functioning as a malware program.

Every person has conversations with themselves so regularly that they aren't even aware that these conversations control their lives. It's a form of hypnosis, and they can't see life any other way. It's a trance they put themselves in that allows them to stay on autopilot. Ownership conversations are the smelling salts of disempowered hypnosis. It wakes us up out of the conversations we've been having with ourselves and then asks the very important question: *Are these conversations getting me where I want to go?*

One tool in your toolbox of shaping the conversations you have with yourself is noticing and choosing the language you use on purpose. While there are many lenses you can use to evaluate your own language, one of our favorites as coaches is the distinction we call "empowered versus disempowered." At any given moment, the language you're using, either out loud or inside your own head, could be described as being "empowered" or "disempowered." I can have a conversation with a person and pretty quickly discover if they're coming from an empowered place or a disempowered place.

DISEMPOWERED LANGUAGE	EMPOWERED LANGUAGE
Maybe	Yes (or No)
I can't	I can
I have to	I get to
I should	I choose to
I'll try	I will (or will not)
I don't know, so I'll stop	I don't know, so I'll find out

When we train people at the institute, we train them how to listen for specific language. When leaders use disempowered language, I say, "Now we have two problems. The first problem is whatever challenge you are facing, and the second problem is the language you are using to address the problem from your disempowered stance." Good leaders will handle their language first, and oftentimes in doing so they will not only solve that problem they're facing but solve fifty other problems created by disempowerment.

Wrestling our addiction to blame isn't always fun, at least at first. But it allows us to discover agency in our lives where before we only saw blame. The reality is, we have more agency than we realize. We just have to go hunting for it. I call it "good will hunting." In other words, learning to look for or hunt for your own "will"—your own power—that you've always had but has been buried beneath blame. When you do this, you exercise agency—choice. When you blame others or circumstances, you admit you are powerless to change and that you have no "will." You're effectively saying, "I have no choice." But when you go out with a proverbial searchlight and look for ways you have agency, you immediately engage in a powerful act. I want to assure you that if you currently blame others and have a number of excuses for your present circumstances, there's still hope.

At any point in time, you can switch gears and go from looking for ways to blame to ways to exercise your will; however, I want to suggest that every minute you spend searching for people and things to blame, you're wasting valuable energy and time when you could be "good will hunting." You could be looking for power that you do not realize you have.

Just like there is a lexicon of disempowerment, there is a lexicon of empowerment. And at the institute, we don't just teach coaches how to listen for blame but how to shift their language toward ownership. Sometimes just shifting your language turns on lights in the home of your soul and sheds some perspective on your reality. You'll find agency—your *good will*—that you didn't realize you had and then use it to create what you currently think is out of your reach.

One of our top coaches, Janet Breitenbach, has used this approach both with her clients and in her own life. Stepping into empowered language has transformed her career and her finances and friendships, but the impact of shifting her language has perhaps had the largest influence on her romantic life.

"For years I talked the same way every other woman in Los Angeles talked about the dating scene," she regularly tells people in our group trainings. "Ladies talk about it like it's such a horrible experience. And I did too. I complained about how 'there were no good men in Los Angeles.' How men were flaky or narcissistic or boring. I didn't realize it at the time, but I was feeding my mind disempowered thoughts that then my brain wanted to be right about. At the firm, we often say, 'More than sex, more than drugs, the human brain wants to be *right*.' So you want to be careful about what you give it to be right about. Every second I spent trying to be right about men in LA was time I was wasting when I could be working to create a relationship that could last a lifetime. My disempowered language was making me critical, cynical, and without me realizing it, was draining me of energy that I needed to show up fully in my life." So she decided to change her language. "I stopped talking like LA was a cesspool for dating, and

I started talking about all the amazing men who were in this town, even though at the time I didn't see them. But I knew they were out there, chasing their dreams, treating people well, looking for someone to love and be loved by. I stopped criticizing myself and why a good man wouldn't want to be with me, and I started valuing myself more. I stopped making fun of dating apps and started asking, 'What does it look like to date with integrity on an app?'"

As she did this, she started making different decisions. She started dating differently. She found agency and willpower she didn't know she had. "Rather than showing up looking for all the ways a man was lacking, I showed up to be present and kind." Her shift in language created a shift in perspective, which helped her to see opportunities when others saw obstacles. It gave her more energy. She started to enjoy the dating process a little more. One day she went on a brief date with a quiet guy in a coffee shop in Silver Lake, a hip enclave of Los Angeles. "After the date, he asked me out again, and I said, 'I don't think it's a good match.' He asked why. Usually, when guys asked why, I'd just lie or say some version of 'it's not you; it's me' to avoid hurt feelings. But I was committed to being honest. So I told him, 'You didn't really ask me very many questions.' To which he replied, 'I'd love another chance.' In my cynical days, I'd say, 'Thanks but no thanks.' But I wasn't who I used to be, so I said yes."

As it turns out, Ryan wasn't quiet at all. He was just a little nervous on the first date.

At least that's what he told me on their wedding day.

In Janet's words, "Changing how I spoke changed how I thought, which changed how I acted, which changed my future forever." Today, along with clients at Nike and coaching some of the most influential people on earth, she enjoys helping people shift from a disempowered to empowered perspective in their romantic lives too. "There are opportunities all around us," she reminded me recently. "We have access to more than we realize we do, if we're only willing to look for it from an empowered place."

She went hunting for her good will, and she found a good man.

Let me ask you: What are the things you long for that, if you were to reflect, how you talk about it is one of the obstacles from getting it? Maybe you long for a raise, but you have little positive things to say about your boss or your work. Maybe you want a relationship, but your language is seeding loneliness instead of love. Maybe you want a better family life or a new career, but your inner dialogue is full of doubt and insecurity or resentment or entitlement. Our language shapes how we see reality. And part of ownership is taking responsibility for our language to be able to see paths to what we want that are currently hidden by language that holds us back.

UNLEASHING THE CREATIVE POTENTIAL OF OWNERSHIP

An ownership mindset is powerful. It has the ability not only to reveal things we can't see but to even *transform* things we don't like into something beautiful.

One night in 1963, in a club in Stuttgart, Germany, Miles Davis, along with some of the best jazz musicians in the world, blew the roof off the place. Ten-time Grammy Award–winning jazz pianist Herbie Hancock tells the story: "Miles Davis and I were performing. Tony Williams was on drums, Ryan Carter was on bass, Wayne Shorter on saxophone. And it was really a hot night—the music was tight, it was powerful, it was innovative, and fun—we were having a lot of fun. The music was *on*."

Hancock continues: "Tony was burning on his drums. And right in the middle of Miles' solos—he was playing one of his amazing solos and I'm trying to keep up and I'm playing—and right in the middle of the solo, I play the wrong chord. A chord that sounded completely wrong. It sounded like a big mistake. And I freaked out—I grimaced and grabbed my own face. And Miles paused."

→ "An ownership mindset is powerful. It has the ability to not only reveal things we can't see but to even transform things we don't like into something beautiful."

One thing you should know about Miles Davis is his reputation for high standards and a quick temper. If you're an aspiring musician, the last person you want to piss off is Miles Davis.

But Miles didn't get angry. He got creative. As Herbie goes on: "Miles paused for less than a second. And then he played some chords that made my chord right—that made it correct. This astounded me. I couldn't believe what I heard. Miles was able to make something that was wrong into something that was right. What I realize now is that Miles didn't hear it as a mistake. He heard it as 'something that happened.' Just an event. And so that was part of the reality of what was happening at that moment. And he dealt with it. He found something. Since he didn't hear it as a mistake, he felt like it was his responsibility to find something that fit. And he was able to do that. That taught me a very big lesson about not only music but about life. We can look for the world to be as we would like it to be as individuals, you know, 'make it easy for me.' We can look for *that*. But I think the important thing is that we grow. And the only way we can grow is to have a mind that is open enough to accept and experience situations as they are and turn them into medicine, turn poison into medicine. Take whatever situation you have and make something constructive happen with it."[5]

All great artists and leaders are able to do this. In a conversation I had with Andy Allo, star of Amazon Video's hit series *Upload*, and who is a gifted coach in her own right and who used to perform with Prince, I asked her, "Did Prince ever make mistakes?" And she responded, "Of course he did, but the thing about Prince is any time he made a mistake, he knew how to make it look like it was how it's supposed to go. So the audience never knew. That's how good he was. He would take whatever was happening and create masterful music."

People who are masters at life are able to take whatever is happening and create something extraordinary from it. Miles and Prince had a choice: they could have blamed others and blamed themselves and told themselves stories about their own and/or their bands' limitations, or they could play the note that was given to them and make it into something incredible.

WHAT TO DO WITH ALL THIS POWER AND CHOICE?

This is the same choice we have in our lives every day, every moment. At any given moment, we get to choose whether we're coming from an empowered or disempowered place. We can choose our language. We can choose to take responsibility for what we're bringing to life rather than waste our time blaming life for what it's not bringing to us. And hopefully in this chapter you've been given some practical ways to both discover the areas of your life where disempowerment might be hiding, as well as how to shift your language from being disempowered to empowered. But one final thing is worth noting in regards to ownership: Owning your power doesn't mean you'll use it in a way that is constructive. Owning your power sometimes can cause more damage than we'd ever imagine.

When you think of great leaders and the most influential minds of the twentieth century, you can't help but think of Nelson Mandela, Martin Luther King Jr., Mahatma Gandhi, and Mother Teresa. What did all four of these people have in common? They all had an incredibly profound multigenerational impact on the world, and they all shared this perspective on personal responsibility. There's a direct correlation between someone's capacity for personal responsibility and their ability to transcend their circumstances in a way that inspires others.

But there is a dark side to this, as many of you astute readers can already predict. There was another leader in the twentieth century who "owned their power."

Adolf Hitler.

Hitler was obsessed with will and personal power. The Nazis would have gigantic private parties and parades among their elite, where they would dress up like Greek gods and celebrate the perceived triumph of their will and power. While there is no doubt that personal responsibility and ownership are tools that can be used to accelerate growth and capacity, that doesn't mean growth and capacity are being used in healthy ways. This is why the multidox approach is so important. Just as vision and growth go together, and ownership is needed for growth, something else is required to keep vision and growth and ownership from being misused. When you step into vision and ownership and growth, you increase your capacity to impact the world. This isn't always a good thing, so now we want you to explore this question: *What is the best way to use all that power?*

Keep reading to find out.

 Want to go deeper on this topic? We've developed free resources for you and your team for each chapter, including discussion questions, recorded interviews with our coaches, and more. To access, scan the QR code or go to www.novus.global/book/chapter7.

CHAPTER 8
BECOMING WORTH FOLLOWING

The best way to find yourself is to lose yourself in the service of others.

→ **MAHATMA GANDHI**

Mind the Gap—The _____ Business—For versus From—There's Something in Your Teeth—Asking for Permission—Who Do You (Not) Love—Calling Others Out—It's a Way of Being, Baby

"You're being an #!&%@."

These are the words of David Gerber, one of our best coaches and partners at the firm. Believe it or not, this is a direct quote of him talking to one of his clients. He is one of the fiercest advocates of his clients I have ever met. I asked him how it felt saying something like that to someone who was paying him money to help them. "I don't use language like that very often," Gerber told me. "My faith is important to me, and I even helped start a church in Berkeley years ago. So it's not like I talk like a drunken sailor or anything.[1] But I also wanted to get through to this guy who I really believed in. I didn't know if it was going to work, but part of coaching is being willing to try anything to break through to someone. After the words left my mouth, I thought, *Oh man, I really, really hope this works*."

His client sat back and let David's words sink in. There was a long pause. Then his client took a deep breath, laughed, and said, "You're right." What followed were months of coaching together, during which David's client grew in ways he never knew he could.

You see, love doesn't always look the way we think it does.

THE LOVE BUSINESS

A few years ago, I was having a conversation with one of my clients who was having the best season of his life so far. He was the CEO of a $3 billion company with offices all around the country. All metrics were up. Leaders were doing "the happy dance" in the hallways from the bonuses they had earned from going above and beyond expectations. It had been a good year. We were reflecting on what was contributing to his success when he told me, "Jason, the more I grow as a leader, the more I realize love is at the center of what I do."

"That's right," I said. "You're in the love business."

Love is one of those words that suffers from what we call "unfamiliarity through overexposure"—meaning that

→ "Love doesn't always look the way we think it does."

sometimes we're exposed to something so often that it starts to lose its meaning. Sometimes we understand love less and less because we talk about it, sing about it, make movies about it, complain about it, and search for it so much.

Love itself is multidoxical. There's rom-com love. There's parent-child love. There's pet love. There's friendship love. There's religious love. And, of course, there's food love.

But what about work love? Obviously, I'm not talking about office romance. I'm not talking about face-to-face love. I'm talking about shoulder-to-shoulder love. Or maybe soldier-to-soldier love. The kind of love infantrymen have after being in the trenches together. The same kind of love athletes develop with each other after going through the highs and lows of competitive sports. Team love.

There's a kind of love for others that can be used anywhere but is especially useful at work. It's not being likable. It's not being nice. It's not being romantic. It's not being soft. It's not avoiding conflict. It's not telling people what they want to hear.

It's something else.

Meta performers define this kind of love as "fierce advocacy." At Novus Global, we are advocating for each other's vision. We are advocating for each other's growth. We are constantly advocating for each other to take ownership of our actions, our lives, so we can all achieve our visions. This kind of love is best expressed by fiercely advocating.

How, you're wondering? By having the courage to show some-one a potentially hard but helpful perspective. By facing difficult situations and confronting conflict in a way that increases their chances of success. By deeply believing in another person's capacity for greatness, even if it's uncomfortable for both of you.

I once had a client laugh and say to me, "Jason, if my wife walked in on one of our sessions, she might think you're abusing me." I asked him why, and he said, "Because I don't let anyone in my life talk to me the way you do." The reason for that is because I get paid to tell my clients what no one else will. I get paid to do or say anything I can to serve them, even if it doesn't necessarily sound "nice." The reason my clients keep coming back isn't just because I'm tough—it's because they know my toughness is coming from a place of fierce advocacy for the things *they say they care about*.

One of the companies we work with, the Rockefeller Group, has agape (divine) love as one of their core values. These days the CEO gives occasional talks to university students to inspire them to consider looking at his chosen career in a new way. He asks them, "What do you think about when you think of real estate? Almost everyone thinks of villains in movies. The bad guy is always a developer—Lex Luther in *Superman*, the bank and developer in *Goonies*." He wants to shift the paradigm and change the story. How? With love. What if real estate was on a mission to help and serve people? And so that's his divine (agape) call. He goes from being a bad guy to being a Blues Brother, on a mission from God. He's on a mission to make real estate and development an act of love. He's become obsessed with the idea of affordable housing and partnering with nonprofits and for-profit developers to solve America's housing crisis.

But it's not simply about having a mission that makes a positive impact in the world. *It's about how he and his team treat each other while fulfilling their mission.* The proof is in the pudding: when we first started coaching him and his team, he said he wanted the employees in the company to love working with each other so much that they'd like their firm to be ranked as one of the top one hundred places to work in New York City. At the time of writing this book, the results just came out: it wasn't in the top one hundred.

It was in the top fifty.

That's the power of love. And they're only getting started.

FOR VERSUS FROM

A couple of years ago, one of our senior partners, Dan Leffelaar, and I were in Cancun with coaches from all over the world to wrestle with the intersection of leadership and coaching frameworks. We had lots of spirited discussions. There were several times when we had a few tense conversations with some of the other coaches. From the outside, they might have looked like heated arguments or even fights. After all, we didn't agree with a lot of what was presented and felt responsible to engage and either see what we were missing or perhaps persuade others to see things from our point of view. After one such conversation, one of the coaches approached Dan privately and said, "You know, even though you and Jason don't shy away from a good fight, I've noticed something about you two."

"What's that?" Dan asked.

"I can tell you're *for* the people here."

That was music to my ears.

This introduces a distinction in our work that we call "for versus from."

You see, too many times in our meetings and relationships we think about what we want *from* people.

"I need this by Friday."

"Can you talk to the developer about that?"

"Make sure you take care of it."

"I want her to do this."

"I wish she didn't do that."

These are all statements *about wanting something from someone.*

But how many times do we sit and reflect about what we want *for* them?

The book *Leadership and Self-Deception: Getting Out of the Box* by the Arbinger Institute uses the metaphor of being inside the box or outside the box. Inside the box is when you are seeing people as obstacles to what you want. Outside the box is when you are seeing them as people with wants and needs and desires of their own.

They give this example: A husband and wife are sleeping, and they hear their baby cry in the next room. The husband wakes up, and he thinks, *I should go. She had an exhausting day, and she was on duty last night. I should go take care of the baby.* But then he thinks again. *Nah.* So there's this moment of self-betrayal. He knows he could or should get up, but he's choosing not to. Then the self-deception starts, because he starts justifying it. *I work hard. I was at work all day. I am the one who pays the bills around here. She doesn't. She doesn't appreciate me as much as she should. Why isn't she getting up?* If you want to get out of the box of self-betrayal and self-deception, you have to be *for* another person's best interest. You have to get out of your own way.

It's true—in the workplace, there's an endless amount of things we want from each other. That's part of the nature of work, especially when working on teams. We all expect things from each other. But what we do in a fierce-advocacy (love) culture or a meta-performing (love) culture is shift that question from *What do I want from somebody?* to *What do I want* for *somebody?*

FROM	FOR
It's about mostly you.	It's about mostly them.
It's about what you want only.	It includes what they want.
When they don't comply, we get resentful.	When they don't comply, we get curious.
We build an adversarial relationship.	We build an advocating relationship.
Tears down.	Lifts up.
Gives feedback to hurt.	Gives feedback to help.
Calling people out.	Calling people forward.
We're clear on our vision only.	We help them get clear on their vision.

That is moving from inside the box to outside the box. When you're inside the box, you're only thinking, *What can I get from this person? What do I want from this person? How is this person not measuring up to me?*

When you're thinking about what you can do for others, you ameliorate whatever situation you're in immediately. It shifts us away from a zero-sum us versus them and toward a more win-win synergy of us for them. You start exploring the question, "How can I become better by helping you become better?"

One of the people who has shaped my thinking on this is former Chick-fil-A executive and one of the best leaders I know, Jeff Henderson. He's the author of the book *Know What You're FOR: A Growth Strategy for Work, An Even Better Strategy for Life*. Years ago he brought in myself and my sister Amanda Jaggard, the cofounder of the Meta Performance Institute, to work with the leaders of one of the organizations he was running. Before we left, he surprised me by handing me an exact replica of Thor's hammer. "Thanks for being *for* our team today," he said as we took a picture together. Because of this moment and countless others, I could always tell Jeff Henderson was an advocate *for* me.

MAKING THE SHIFT

Here is a powerful question for reflection: *Who do you lead but do not love?* Who is frustrating you on your team right now? Maybe it's your boss, a colleague, or someone who reports to you. Maybe it's a vendor or a client. Ask yourself: What do you want for them? Notice how asking that question changes your energy toward them and opens up creative potential solutions to your frustration you didn't see before.

This is, to quote Huey Lewis and the News twice in one chapter, "the power of love." Being for others actually unleashes energy and creativity that lies latent in the human spirit, on teams, and in companies and communities.

Whenever I'm frustrated with somebody on my team, I'll open up an Evernote file and ask, "What do I want for this person?" Then I'll just write out some things I want for them.

I want them to be successful.

I want them to be happy.

I want them to have *X*, *Y*, and *Z*.

I want this to be the best job they've ever had.

I want them to be able to send their kids to college.

This doesn't mean I can't still ask for the email or project or for them to close their mouths when they eat. It doesn't mean I can't still say, "Hey, I want to talk about this thing that didn't get done." It doesn't mean I can't still say, "Hey, we need to have a hard conversation."

But now the lens from which I view them is different. Now the lens isn't one of entitlement or one of resentment. The lens isn't even one of frustration. Now the lens is one of generosity, even if it's a difficult form of generosity to give.

ON GENEROSITY

I love people who are connoisseurs of something. People who love wine or cigars or sports cars or music or food. There's something life-giving about exploring the depths of a thing. Of giving yourself permission to totally geek out on something and to find other people who love the same things you do.

Of all the things to be a connoisseur of, generosity is one of them. I often tell the leaders I work with and spend time around, "I want to be a connoisseur of generosity. I want to be good at generosity the way Picasso was good at painting."

Consequently, our firm and institute are obsessed with generosity, so much so that we talk about it all the time and are working on another book featuring generosity as a value that informs and shapes GO LIVE. As a way of helping our community and our clients explore all the avenues of generosity, we developed the acronym ROCKET to help people understand just how many ways there are to be generous toward others.

Relationships: What are the relationships I have that could also be a gift to others?

Opportunities: What opportunities do I hold that I can give to others for their growth?

Cash: How can I support other people financially and do that in an intelligent way?

Knowledge: How can I share what I know to help others be successful?

Energy: How can I encourage, inspire, and draw out others' best energy?

Time: How can I give my time to serve others so they can win faster?

Most of the time when people think of *generosity* they think of money. The ROCKET acronym helps remind us that money is only one of many ways we can be generous toward others. And many times money isn't the most valuable thing we can give.

In fact, one of the most powerful forms of generosity you can give at work is feedback.

GENEROUS FEEDBACK

One of the most powerful ways to fiercely advocate for others is through feedback. Who among us hasn't received or given feedback? Almost everyone I informally poll during trainings raises their hand when I ask, "How many of you have given or received feedback, and it didn't go well?" In our workplaces and world, we're always giving and receiving feedback. And when it comes to performance and better-performing cultures, we are constantly talking about getting more done in less time or reinventing ourselves to become more extraordinary. It's simply impossible to grow at that speed without feedback. Meta performance can only happen when we get feedback from others.

That being said, I know there are a lot of us who have wanted to give feedback to help another person grow faster but were afraid because we suspected it would not be well received. Right now there are people in your world who you care about, and there's feedback you could give them that would help them grow. But chances are you might not be giving it. Without feeling guilty or shaming yourself, I want you to notice how that might be robbing that person of the information they need to grow.

There are two types of feedback that are really helpful for me. First, there's feedback I've never heard before. Someone's alerted me to an unconscious behavior or activity I had no idea I was doing. My response is usually, "Oh, that's really helpful. Thank you so much. I've never thought about that before."

Then there is the feedback that people give me that I knew about already, but I didn't know they knew! When someone else mentions that kind of feedback to me, it makes it more real. And because it's "out there," now I am more likely to do something about it. It's like they've helped me stop avoiding it. They've done me a favor, which goes back to this simple idea of being *for* people. It has fundamentally changed how I see people, how I lead them, and how I respond to them. When I have tough conversations, it helps me stay rooted in love for that person, even if the conversation doesn't go the way either of us want it to.

THE SECRET TO GREAT FEEDBACK

When we do trainings, we have a "Five Steps for Giving Powerful Feedback" process. But really there's one step that is the most important.

But before I tell you what it is, I need to introduce it with a story.

I'm pretty introverted. I'll go to parties, but it really helps if I can have a wingman who is way more social than I am. One particular time I went to a cocktail party—where they had drinks and a "fancy" salad bar—with one of my best friends. There's something really fun about working a room with someone who knows what they're doing in social situations, and she knew what she was doing. We would walk into a room and "small talk" divide and conquer, with just about everyone in the room. There'd be times when we were side by side, and other times when we'd be on opposite ends of the room. We'd make eye contact, and I'd smile because it was fun to watch her do her extrovert thing. After we had spent the entire night talking to everyone in the room, we got in the car to leave. As I looked in the rearview mirror to adjust it, I smiled at my reflection, and as soon as I did, that's when I saw it.

There was a gigantic piece of salad in my teeth.

It wasn't a little "oh, don't mind me; I'm just hiding in the crevice of your gums" fleck of salad. No. I am talking about an NFL mouthguard spinach grill covering almost all my teeth. You could have windsailed with this thing.

And the first thought that came to my mind, which is the first thought that comes to a lot of people's minds in similar situations, was: I'd been around my "friend" the entire night. I've been around hundreds of people laughing, smiling, talking *the entire night*.

Why didn't somebody say something?

Would it have been embarrassing if someone early in the night, after I had eaten the offending greenery, said, "Hey, buddy" with the universal gesture for "there's something in your teeth—go check yourself"? Perhaps. I'd be embarrassed for a moment, but wouldn't it have been better to feel that momentary flash of embarrassment and then fix it rather than walk around with a green mouth all night? When someone tells us we have something in our teeth or have toilet paper stuck to our shoe or our fly is down, our immediate response—after the twinge of embarrassment—is deep gratitude. We say, "Thank you!" We know that the person who told us is a true friend, because nobody wants to be the one walking around looking like a fool. (To prove it, you have probably checked your clothes and rubbed your tongue along your teeth while reading this, just to be safe). We can all agree that no one wants food stuck in their teeth in social settings. Put another way: we all share the same vision.

Which leads me to my point: the most important part of feedback is giving it in a way that aligns with the person's vision.

When you give feedback, make sure you align it with what the other person wants. Most of the time, when we give feedback, we align the feedback with *our* vision and what it can do for us. But the best feedback aligns with *their* vision for *their* lives, not just yours. Everybody has a vision of looking good at a cocktail party. Nobody wants to have their pants zipper down. Nobody wants to have toilet paper stuck to their shoes or dress. Nobody wants to have something in their teeth. Their vision is for them to be seen and perceived a certain way. And we all kind of intuitively know this.

Companies have vision statements. Leaders have vision statements for themselves. Oftentimes we're clear. While High performers are always clear about their vision for their lives, Meta performers are clear about visions that *other* people have for their lives. I carry in my heart the vision my chief of staff has for her future. I know she's an artist. I know she loves film, like I do, and music. I know she loves the leadership stuff we're doing now. But that's not the nuclear thing for her. There are other things she wants to do with her future. I don't know when that's going to happen. I don't know how that's going to happen. But I have that in me. I know what the vision is for my team members. I carry around with me what they want. And as I exist in the world, I'm always thinking, *How can I make getting what I want help them get what they want? How can we align our visions?* Oftentimes I'll be in rooms with senior-level executives, and I'll say, "Raise your hand if you have a vision for your life." All of them raise their hands.

→ "Most of the time, when we give feedback, we align the feedback with our vision and what it can do for us. But the best feedback aligns with their vision for their lives, not just yours."

Then I'll say, "Raise your hand if you know the visions of the people you lead." Hardly anybody raises their hands.

It is incredibly difficult to give feedback if you don't know what the other person wants.

The clearer you are about another person's vision, the more you can look for the alignment of your vision and theirs when you're giving feedback.

WITHHOLDING FEEDBACK ISN'T LOVE

Do you want good things for the people around you? Oftentimes, in "soft-love" cultures—usually not high-performing cultures—people think they're not going to have the needed conversation with someone, because they "love them." They're not going to have a feedback conversation with so-and-so, because they don't want to "hurt them." And while that may look like love, it's actually the opposite of love.

	BEING FOR SOMEONE	BEING AGAINST SOMEONE
GIVING FEEDBACK	Fierce Advocacy	Adversarial
WITHHOLDING FEEDBACK	People-Pleasing	Indifferent

It's hard to make the case for "love" when there's feedback you could give someone to help them be successful, but you don't. When you choose not to be helpful. When you choose not to serve them. You're going to let them walk around with the proverbial kale in their teeth because you don't want to hurt them. Let me tell you: Withholding that feedback, not fiercely advocating for their growth, is going to cost them. And it's going to cost you and your team or company or community, all because you don't want to cause a moment of discomfort. That is not love.

When you think about it, withholding feedback is a bit like lying. It's also a form of manipulation, especially when you're withholding feedback that could really help somebody. It can also a form of antagonism. One of the greatest challenges leaders face is leading people who are more talented than them. There is a fear among some leaders that "If I give people feedback, what if they get so good that they don't need me anymore?" So we withhold feedback because, deep down inside, we don't want others to leave us behind.

The key to meta performing cultures is to learn how to give feedback rooted in love and to become strong enough to receive any kind of feedback. Clinical psychologist and leadership coach Henry Cloud has one of my favorite quotes: before you can do anything well, you have to give yourself permission to do it poorly. This is especially true when it comes to feedback. While obviously you don't want to abuse anyone, I highly recommend you and the people you lead and love practice learning about each other's visions and then simply solicit each other's perspectives on how you might be getting in your own respective ways of achieving those visions. At the firm and the institute, we regularly are asking for and offering feedback. Weekly we are getting it "wrong" and asking for forgiveness and growth in how we help each other win. But we're also getting better at it. And our people are growing faster. And that is worth the risk."

LOVE THE GAP

One final note about love as it pertains to meta performance . Once you're clear on a vision for the future that really excites you, the kind that demands you grow, take ownership, and reinvent yourself in order to accomplish it, then it will become obvious that where you want to go isn't where you are now.

In other words, as soon as you create a vision, you also create a gap.

Most people relate to gaps in their lives with shame. It can be really painful to feel like our lives don't match our vision. In fact, the reason many of us don't try to grow or take ownership of our current reality is shame, which results from fear. And this fear-based shame keeps us in a holding pattern of sorts, invariably widening the gap between where we are and where we want to be.

But there are three tactics we employ to try to decrease the gap. First, our response to any shame around a gap in our lives is to simply decrease the size of our vision. We often call this "settling." We keep our lives small, and we try not to improve things too much. The second thing we do to decrease the gap is inflate our current reality. This helps us feel like we're moving toward the gap superficially. We pretend or romanticize our current situation. Have you ever assumed you had more in your savings account, only to find out you're nearly overdrawn? Have you ever hopped on a scale and discovered you weighed way more than you thought? Many of us inflate how much money we earn, or say we work out seven days a week and eat only vegetables and fruits, but our lives and activities—and bodies and bank accounts—don't reflect that reality. Our minds have a propensity to exaggerate things in order to feel like we're growing when we're not.

But it's not real. It's fake. Secretly, we know this, which causes us to feel shame, and the cycle continues.

The third way to lessen the gap is to *actually* close the gap. Interestingly, many high performers who do this are motivated by shame. Shame is one of the best motivators for high performers. I can't tell you how many people I meet who are just phenomenally accomplished. And if you ask them why they're so good at what they do, invariably, the cause is rooted in shame or fear. In fact, that's one of the reasons why many people don't like the word *performance*. They may have traumatic memories of learning to play piano at eight years old and being asked to "perform" in front of all their parents' friends when they weren't ready to or didn't want to. I had a friend who was a competitive judo champion. When he was young and lost a match, his father would physically beat him. He became a high performer at judo mostly out of fear of losing because it would result in his father's wrath. While this technically "works" it obviously comes with huge costs. You become stressed, burned out, and frequently feel overcome or overwhelmed. You suffer from perfectionism and self-inflicted criticism. Nothing's ever good enough. You're never satisfied with your work or anyone else's. You become trapped in a spiral of shame and fear, and you can't move beyond the high-performance and shame cycles.

What's important to take from this chapter is that whenever you experience a gap in your life, shame isn't the only emotion you can experience. If you're a first-year med student and don't have a degree, you're not allowed to operate on anyone. You don't have a specialization yet, let alone know where the cafeteria is. There's a massive gap between where you are and where you want to be. But you don't walk around with your tail between your legs. You don't walk around ashamed. You don't worry about people saying, "You're a first-year; what's wrong with you?" Instead, you say, "Yeah, of course I'm a first-year. I'm new here. I'm exactly where I'm supposed to be." That's true for most people on the first day of school or at a new job. They don't experience shame. They're excited, maybe a little nervous. There's hope. There is optimism. That's not fear. That's love.

We call it "loving the gap."

WHEN THE GAPS GET REAL

"I don't think you can be a leader and not love being in the gap." These are words from Stephen Jeffs, the CEO of Network Solutions, an Australian-based company that employs thousands of people across the Southern Hemisphere. I met Stephen in 2017 during a season of work when I was traveling to Australia several times a year, working with various leaders there. We hit it off, and our firm got to work with them for several years doing trainings and coaching with their key leaders.

The three primary values for Network Solutions might sound strange to some. They are as follows: vision, faith, and love. So, when they got exposed to our "Love the Gap" methodology, it resonated with them immediately. Stephen told me, "We made shirts and screen savers and smartphone wallpapers all saying 'Love the Gap.' Six years later it's still a dominant theme of our culture. It's become one of those statements that I can throw out to my team, and they know exactly what I'm talking about."

Network Solutions is a sales-based organization, and often they have very aggressive sales goals placed on them by their larger partners. Oftentimes the sales goals are beyond what the team thinks they can do. "When that happens we have two choices," says Jeffs. "We can blame or get defensive, or we can step in and step up and own the gap and learn to love the opportunity to grow. As our culture continues to embrace the idea of loving the gap, there have been several times when we've not only hit the sales metrics that have been placed on us but have exceeded them, surprising even us."

Put another way: *they didn't know they could do that.*

"I'm a massive believer that love can be the foundation of business," Stephen said. "And if you do that, it actually creates the best results."

I couldn't have said it better myself.

CALLING YOU FORWARD

During one of our trainings with Network Solutions, Amanda Jaggard was in Australia with me, and we were coaching and training together—in our companies, we try to do everything in pairs or trios as much as possible, whether it's workshops, public speaking, or even podcasts. During the training, I noticed Amanda wasn't doing something she usually does that brings a lot of value. I felt like she wasn't bringing that part of her best, so I brought it to her attention. Her response wasn't defensive. It was simply, "Thanks for calling me out." And she meant it.

I responded, "I didn't call you out. I called you forward."

That's what fierce advocacy does. It calls us forward. It doesn't diminish us. It's expansive. It's creative. Calling someone out is shame-based and punitive; however, calling people forward is love-based, future-based, hope-based.

There's an ancient proverb that says, "Perfect love casts out fear."[2] You cannot be a meta performer without love. Meta performers are meant to go places that can only be sustained by love

→ "Calling someone out is shame-based and punitive. Calling people forward is love-based, future-based, hope-based."

because you cannot continually reinvent yourself sustainably if you're being motivated by guilt, fear, and shame. Fear and love are both nuclear. But while fear destroys you, love can become a nearly limitless source of energy for you.

And that's what we're going to talk about next.

 Want to go deeper on this topic? We've developed free resources for you and your team for each chapter, including discussion questions, recorded interviews with our coaches, and more. To access, scan the QR code or go to www.novus.global/book/chapter8.

CHAPTER 9

TENDING TO THE FIRE

We will either find a way, or make one.

→ HANNIBAL BARCA, CIRCA 160 BCE

The Legend of Andrew Ladd—Can't Hurt Me—Usher's Producer Loves to Sail—"Work Hard Play Hard" Is Stupid—LeBron's Nap Times—The Mayor of Nike—What to Do with Extra Energy

"I lost my fire."

This is Andrew Ladd, a professional hockey player for the Arizona Coyotes, in a conversation with me and his coach, director of Novus Global Sport Dan Leffelaar. He was describing to me the time when he started to fall out of love with a game he'd excelled at all his life.

Ladd isn't just any hockey player; he is also a two-time Stanley Cup winner. But through a series of injuries, he had found himself back in the minor leagues. After years of playing hard and pushing himself competitively, he wondered if his career as a professional hockey player was over.

He felt like he had nothing left to give.

He had lost his energy. He was tired. He was, in his own words, "distant and stuck in his own head." But like many professional athletes and high performers who had pushed themselves for years in their chosen careers, he couldn't identify or understand what was happening.

Luckily, during a long car ride with another athlete, he was referred to Dan, who was already working with several NHL players. At the time, Ladd was at a low point and recovering from two knee surgeries. What had served Andrew well as a young person—brutally pushing himself beyond his physical limits—wasn't working anymore. He wasn't so sure he had anything left in the tank, let alone another gear.

In working with Dan, he realized he had forgotten somewhere along the way that hockey wasn't just a career; it was also *a game*. Sure, it was a tough game. One of the toughest games in the world. Pucks fly across the ice moving at speeds over one hundred miles per hour. Two-hundred-pound athletes slam into each other at over twenty miles per hour. Anything can happen. But there's also nothing like it. That's why it could also be, well, *fun*. It could be energizing and yet he had fallen out of love with it. And like many relationships on the rocks, he wasn't so sure he could fall back in love. How could he regain the energy that had sustained him through the early, hard-driving days of his career?

WHEN YOU THINK YOU HAVE NOTHING LEFT

Ladd's story is similar to a lot of high performers. They're burned out. They think they don't have anything left in the tank, but in reality they still have access to more energy than they realize. David Goggins—ultramarathoner, Navy SEAL, and author of *Can't Hurt Me*—argues that you are far more capable than you think you are: "When your mind is telling you you're done, you're really only 40 percent done." You have it in you; you're just not aware of it. Or, more accurately, you're so focused on what's going wrong that you can't see what's going right.

Most pregnant women are familiar with what is called "mommy brain"—brain fog, memory lapses, feeling spaced out, forgetful, and just downright out of it. It's easy for mothers to get caught up in the idea that they might be becoming "dumber" or are no longer at the "top of their game." In fact, the opposite is true. In the book *The Mommy Brain: How Motherhood Makes Us Smarter*, author Katherine Ellison argues that scientific research demonstrates that pregnancy enhances senses, increases awareness, and improves memory skills, so mothers can multitask better and

> → "When your mind is telling you you're done, you're really only 40 percent done."
> —David Goggins

take bolder risks while becoming more empathetic and adept at negotiating on behalf of their offspring. These advantages help women as mothers as well as in their work and social lives. It seems when women are the hardest on themselves, they are, in fact, at the top of their game. They're twice as capable as they've ever been. It's just that the game difficulty *tripled*. The temptation is to become so focused on arguing for their own limitations that they forget they have access to more energy than they've ever had in their lives.

And like them, you have more energy available to you than you think. This chapter is about how you find it.

TWO APPROACHES TO ENERGY

When it comes to energy, I like to say there are usually two types of people: sailors and rowers.

A sailor's natural inclination is to orient themselves toward where they have innate momentum. They may ask, "Where are the doors opening? What is the path of least resistance?" They love for things to be natural. They "go with the flow." They see a world filled with opportunities. They make choices based on what's exciting them. Sailors do an excellent job of designing their life around things that excite them and energize them. Words that sailors will often use to describe situations are "feels expansive," "fun," and "enjoyable." Sailors are great at tapping into energy systems that are already there. They "harness the wind" that's already blowing.

One of my favorite examples of a master sailor is Chris North. He is one of our top coaches at the firm and is on the faculty at the Meta Performance Institute. Beneath his tough "wanna fight?" exterior, he actually has the heart of an artist and mystic. Years ago, before he became one of our partners in the firm, Chris hired me to coach him, and he described his life as a roller coaster of success, and not always the good kind. "Money would just run through my fingers. I'd make millions, and then I'd spend millions." It wasn't like he was flushing his money away on drugs and gambling. He was (and is) an entrepreneur who had started several successful companies, including a production company that won an MTV Music Award and has worked with artists like Rihanna, Usher, and Selena Gomez. He knew how to do quality work and how to work hard. It's just that it was always feast or famine. This is a classic sailor. When the wind blew, Chris knew how to hoist his sail and catch it, surfing the raging wind wildly like Lieutenant Dan during a thunderstorm in *Forrest Gump*. But then, as with all storms, the wind would stop. The momentum would be gone, and eventually so would the revenue, until the next gust of wind came along—and when you're good, it always comes. Chris is an expert sailor, so he knew how to make the most of the wind. But if the wind wasn't blowing, Chris was struggling. "At the time I felt like I was just wired that way," Chris told me in a recent conversation reflecting on that season of his life. "And I was entitled. I felt like the world owed it to me for the wind to blow." Because Chris was so good at sailing, he could have lived the rest of his life this way. Most sailors do.

If Chris's story represents a classic sailor, Andrew Ladd's story represents the classic rower. In contrast to sailing, rowers *make* things happen. They aren't waiting for the wind to blow. Strong current? No problem, they have the muscle to row against it. They love words like *hard work, grit, resilience,* and *sweat.* If sailors are hoisting sails and sitting back, feeling the wind, rowers are gripping their ores tight, plunging them into the heavy water and forcing progress, with or without the wind. Rowers don't see something worth doing unless it's hard. They climb mountains because they are there. Rowers are great at *creating* energy when there isn't any around them. Just like Walter White in "Breaking Bad" who famously said, "I *am* the danger." Rowers don't look for energy. They *are* the energy.

Until, of course, they're not. That's when they burn out.

So sailors are always looking for the open door. Rowers like to kick doors down.

I want to be clear: Neither is right or wrong. Neither is better than the other. Sailing is about catching the momentum. Rowing is about creating momentum. They are simply different ways of orienting yourself toward energy. The sailor is looking to harness energy outside themselves (and there is a lot of energy out there to be harnessed). The rower is looking to harness the energy inside them (and there is a lot of energy inside as well). Both are also equally important when it comes to achieving your goals. The wind isn't always blowing, so sailors are going to need to row. And if rowers don't learn to listen for the wind, they are going to burn out and get exhausted. Most high performers (like all people) have a preference for either sailing or rowing and tend to judge the other style of energy management. Rowers judge sailors for not working hard. Sailors judge rowers for trying to force everything. And when the wind stops, the sailors complain that their luck or opportunities have run out. Or maybe it was God. There is nothing they can do. Conversely, rowers collapse from exhaustion and make little progress, even when the wind is blowing. Like those who can relate to Andrew Ladd, eventually all that arduous work ceases to be fun, and they don't think they have anything left to give. Either way, you have the potential to lose momentum if you're only drawing on one type of energy. Rowers are so busy rowing that they don't stop and listen for the wind. And sailors are so busy gliding along, they never learn to row and their muscles atrophy.

The only way to go as fast and as far as possible is to become adept at both. What separates high performers from meta performers is that they are *both expert sailors and diligent rowers.* Take Chris: for

→ "What separates high performers from meta performers is that they are both expert sailors and diligent rowers."

Chris, joining the firm was an act of rowing. Sailors don't always like being on teams. They don't like doing things just because other people are doing them. Sailors aren't *followers*. But Chris had a sense that he could go further faster with others than on his own as a coach and entrepreneur. A year after he joined the firm, his life and way of being had radically changed. His coaching practice grew. His clientele became some of the most respected entertainers in the world. Even his countenance changed. He seemed happier, more powerful, but more joyful. One time we were hanging out with a bunch of coaches from the firm and someone asked Chris, "What's gotten into you?" And Chris responded, gesturing to the team, "You did." It's not that Chris stopped sailing; it's that he put his ores into the waters of a community that had a value for rowing. And his success of sailing while rowing has been phenomenal.

And then there's Andrew: he was a classic rower. When in doubt, try harder. Skate faster. More Sweat. But with Dan as his coach, Ladd flipped the script. What if, Dan suggested, Andrew redesigned his relationship to hockey?

SAILOR	ROWER
Wind	Work
Look for open doors	Kick doors down
Ease	Effort
Intuitive	Intentional
Miracles	Make it happen
Mystical	Tactical
Trust	Boldness
Breeze	Sweat
When the stars align	Reach for the stars
Wander	Build
Listen	Act
Sense	Move
Request	Declare
Emotion	Commitment
How you're wired	What you choose

What if he could just go out and *play*? What if he could relax? What if he could return to what made hockey fun in the first place? Could he skate out on the ice and use the skills he had honed over the years and make it a game again? Dan had Andrew remember what it was like in the past, when he used to play for the love of the game. They also practiced imagining Andrew's preferred future. Andrew (then a minor league player) imagined himself playing in the NHL again. He saw himself reaching the elusive one-thousand-game milestone. These visions seemed impossible, yet the new goal *energized* him. His game almost instantly improved. In the process, he also discovered something he had lost on his way up the proverbial mountain—he *loved* hockey. He *really* loved it. He was learning to sail again.

Andrew eventually made it back to the NHL. But that's not all. In April 2022, he became one of the rarified NHL players to play his one thousandth game. For some perspective on how difficult this is, think of it this way: A young hockey player has a one in four thousand chance of playing in the NHL.[1] Of those who make it to the NHL, only 1 out of 20 make it over one thousand games. In the hundred-plus year history of the NHL, Andrew Ladd is the 357th player to ever play one thousand games. The vision he created for himself, even in the darkest and lowest times of his career, came to fruition. In an interview with a writer for the Arizona Coyotes, Andrew said, "I was sitting in Bridgeport a couple of years ago with this goal in mind to get back to playing NHL games again and hitting this milestone. To finally be here and see all that hard work and time that I put into getting back into this spot so I could have this opportunity is fulfilling, to say the least."[2]

To say the least.

A meta performer does the work, and they know when to let things work for them. They do all the heavy lifting required to get a job done. And then they listen for the wind and learn how to hoist their sail. And being a sailor doesn't get you off the hook of preparing for opportunities. In fact, the better sailor you become, the better rower you need to be.

I want you to pause and ask yourself:

Do you tend to be more like a sailor or a rower?

Have you had to fight and claw your way to the top?

Or do you always seem to land in the right environment, where you can thrive?

Is this a sailing season or a rowing season? For you? For your team?

A friend of mine recently was thinking about getting a new job. As soon as he put out the word that he was looking, five companies became interested in hiring him. He didn't have to really work for it. The sailor often has their pick of available suitors. Naturally, sailors take what's available. That may not seem like a big problem to have, until it is. I said to my friend, "I understand that all these companies are after you, and that your instinct is to pick the best of those approaching you. What I'm wondering is, can you look beyond all that and instead ask yourself: What is your ideal job that no one is currently offering you? What's the job that feels a little bit out of your league?" Of course, this would require him to adopt a rower mentality. He'd have to start kicking some doors down. Coaching a sailor is partly about building up a pain tolerance and giving them permission to go after things that look hard or impossible and then teaching them how to work hard for it. The sailor will maximize their sailing when they find things worth rowing for. Coaching rowers is different. When you're coaching rowers, you give them permission to find ways to make things effortless. Fun. Enjoyable. Andrew Ladd had been rowing so hard, for so long, he had forgotten how to have fun. So he, like maybe some of you, had to relearn how to enjoy himself. Everything is going to be okay if you take a day off. It's okay to put the oars down. How can we make this fun again? You don't have to turn everything into a struggle.

TENDING TO THE FIRE

We typically work with people who *think* they are burned out, but possibly aren't. The two most common causes of burnout are people either a) ignoring the wind that's blowing around them and b) rowing with their oars out of the water. The former needs to learn to access the energy that's around them and within them. The latter needs to redirect their energy toward progress and away from busyness.

Either way, we call this tending to the fire.

One day on Nike's legendary campus, a game of tag erupted between thousands of the employees. For a brief moment in time, one of the most successful companies in the history of the world transformed into a blacktop playground at recess time. The man who was responsible? Kevin Carroll. Kevin Carroll is one of the most interesting people I've ever met in my life and he is a master of harnessing energy. I once saw him kick a ball from the stage into the balcony of a sold-out audience in an Opera Hall. His talk got a standing ovation. He served in the US Air Force for ten years in military intelligence. The founder and CEO of Nike, Phil Knight, called him the "Mayor of Nike." And one of the most important questions he asks himself every day is, "How do I take care of myself properly to show up for others?" He calls your presence your "spark," and he always reminds me, "You've got to bring your spark."

Recently, when he was working with our team, he said, "You have to replenish your own energy source so you have energy to give to others." In other words, you have to tend to the fire you have. One of the ways Kevin does this is through various energy rituals he engages in before going into meetings, getting on stage, and even starting the day. "When I work out, it's not about getting buff," Kevin says. "It's about getting my energy right."

"I've done a lot of work with Native American communities," Kevin told us. "And they have ceremonies to prepare for an important moment and/or protect their spirit. They'd do different things before they'd go into battle like 'smudging.' They would 'smudge'[their bodies] before any important moment. And so I've developed my own 'smudging' rituals."

If you watch Kevin before he speaks, you'll always see him tap his pocket twice, tap his hat once, and then do the sign of the cross. "The hat represents my grandfather," Kevin told us. "In my pocket, I keep a picture of my grandmother, who I adored, and a picture of my best friend's mom, who was my biggest encourager and made a huge impact on me, and so I always have these two angels in my pocket. And then I cross myself to humble myself, to acknowledge that I'm not doing this on my own, and to always be grateful to share my gift with others again. These rituals ground me." He even wears the same kind of sneakers—in case you're wondering, Chuck Taylors or AJ1s—every time he speaks.

At one point, Kevin got to work with Kobe Bryant, and he said it was fascinating learning about the rituals Kobe developed to help him get his head and heart in a place to compete at the highest possible level. "He came out onto the court a certain way for the layup line. And before he's announced and goes out onto the court it looked like he was flossing with his sneakers but he was actually untying and tying them again and he's saying to himself 'tighten up.' And those types of rituals helped flip a switch for Kobe for him to do what he was able to do."

These are rituals that ground Kevin and Kobe into who they're committed to being.

Tending to your energy is a bit of a paradox. You want to tend to it as if it was finite, but then you want to learn how to create it as if it were infinite. And you want to stand in and inhabit that tension. We spend most of our time thinking, what do I do with the energy I have? Very few people can answer this question:

What would you do if you had twice as much energy?

Do you have trouble imagining this?

This is where vision comes in.

Most people try to pick a vision commensurate with their current energy level versus selecting an energy level that is proportionate to whatever vision they're committed to. When Andrew was recovering from surgery, he didn't have the energy to play one game, let alone his one thousandth NHL game. How did he get that energy?

He *envisioned* himself playing his one thousandth game, and that energized him.

Now it's your turn.

What vision do you have for yourself that would require an extraordinary amount of energy to achieve?

What are the activities you enjoy doing?

How can you design your life as much as possible around achieving that energizing vision?

If you've done all this, and you're still struggling to maintain your energy, the next question to ask is:

Are you resting?

→ "Tending to your energy is a paradox. You want to tend to it as if it were finite, but then you want to learn how to create it as if it were infinite."

ALWAYS REST; NEVER COAST

The fear most people have when it comes to growth is burning out or blowing up. "Don't put more on my plate; I've already got more than I can handle." Or sometimes we do it to ourselves: "I overcommitted, and now I'm paying for it." Two quick thoughts on that: one, in the words of Tom Bilyeau, "You can always slow down." In fact, it's a lot easier to slow down than speed up. Most people, even high performers, don't suffer from going too fast. They suffer from going fast *poorly*. They don't realize that one of the most indispensable tools of speed is rest.

Pop quiz part 2 (part 1 was in chapter 3 about Steve Martin and Martin Short): Who of the following are most likely to sleep for *twelve hours a day*:

a lazy teenager

a person who just completed an ironman

LeBron James

All of the above

One of these probably stuck out as a surprise. It makes sense that teenagers sleep forever. It makes sense for someone who just completed an ironman (like David Gerber from our firm did a few years ago). But it might surprise you that Emmy Award–winning and record-breaking, championship-winning, NBA superstar LeBron James sleeps *twelve hours a day*.

Of course, you could argue that when you get paid $9,700 for every minute you're alive you can afford to sleep twelve hours a day.[3] But that's not why he does it. He does it because that's the kind of rest that's needed for him to perform at a level no one else does over a time frame longer than most NBA athletes. The principle becomes clear: your rate of rest needs to pace your rate of growth.

That's why we like to say, "Always rest; never coast." Part of the journey of meta performance is discerning when you're resting and when you're coasting, and to learn how to rest well so you can get back to the good stuff of growing in an enjoyable (and sustainable) way. I want to ask you some key questions when it comes to rest:

What is more intentional in your life right now: trying to grow or learning to rest?

COASTING	RESTING
Stop working because you don't want to work.	Stop working as a part of a healthy work/rest rhythm.
Doesn't want to go back to work.	Excited to go back to work.
No vision for growth. "I have to work so I can pay for a break."	Vision for how rest plays into growth. "I choose to work and rest."
Desperate for a break.	Could work more, but chooses not to in order to honor the long-term rhythm.
Prisoner, Mercenary, Missionary.	Athlete.
Low-Performer, Performer, High-Performer Mindsets.	Meta-Performance Mindset.
Work Hard, Play Hard.	Work well, Rest Well.
Fear of work.	Joy of work.
Work break is full on non-rejuvenating.	Work break is well designed to rejuvenate.
Used to avoid growth.	Used as part of growth.

How can you leverage resting like a pro so you can grow like a pro?

Meta performance requires meta rest. Trying to do one without the other is a recipe for disaster.

One of my least favorite high-performer sayings is "work hard, play hard." I'm all for hard work. And I'm all for play (though "playing hard" usually means doing something that damages your body in some way #yolo). But I'm more about working well, playing well, and resting well. If you learn to work well, work becomes play. And if you learn to play well, rest becomes essential.

BUILDING A FURNACE

Finally, when tending a fire, you want to make sure you (or someone else) isn't throwing water on it. You want to protect it. You want to build a furnace. A furnace provides two functions, and one of those functions is to protect the fire. You do this by asking:

What activities are currently doing where you feel de-energized after?

What people are you currently hanging out with where you feel de-energized after?

What environments are you currently in where you feel de-energized after?

When you feel de-energized, there is one source and one choice. The source of a lack of energy is always internal. You're de-energized because of how you're relating to whatever it is you're doing. That's what the chapter on ownership is all about. You are the one source. And now you have a choice: do you want to change how you relate to whatever is de-energizing you or do you want to change your proximity to whatever is de-energizing you?

The reality is, you have more energy than you think and you can architect your life into one that produces more energy. This is the second function of a furnace: not simply to keep the fire safe but to help the fire grow.

When I have days that are really busy, but it feels like I'm not making any progress, I feel instantly de-energized. But on days when I feel like everything we're doing is moving me or our company forward, I feel very excited. It feels like I could could work for hours, nearly endlessly.

An expert I respect told me one time that time management is really energy management. And one of the best ways to manage your energy is to ask this question: what is motivating me in this season of my life? Our firm actually developed a motivation assessment we used internally for years called the 5i Assessment (we've since made it available for free to anyone).[4] We wanted to better understand what the team motivators were in order to better lead them and create unique paths to success based on what was exciting them, what they were valuing. The 5i Assessment allows you to measure your current motivational cocktail and leverage your unique motivational makeup in this season of your life. Notice I'm saying "in this season of your life" and not "what motivates you all or most of the time." Our motivations tend to drift and change as we navigate life over the decades, so we wanted to create an assessment that reflected and honored that kind of fluidity.

By the way, assessments are more "sailing" methods of managing energy. Trying to see how people are naturally "wired" so they can more effortlessly tap into it is a sailing strategy. This is an important way to access energy because who wants to be fighting against the wind all the time, against their most habitual ways of showing up in the world?

But a good leader is also going to train people to generate their *own* energy. Everyone has energy. It's there. If you say you don't have it, what you're saying is you don't have the tools to access it. You are responsible for the energy you bring to the room. And it's your job to manage your energy, no matter how you're wired or the distractions, people, or obstacles that get in your way. Many people adopt rituals to access or harness this energy like Kevin Carroll did before giving his speeches. He then drew on that wellspring of energy he'd created while he gave his speeches. His energy was contagious. It had the capacity to light the whole room on fire.

WHAT TO DO WHEN YOU HAVE "TOO MUCH" ENERGY

What happens when you have too much energy?

This question might seem ridiculous at first glance. Who would admit to such a thing? Most people run on empty or more-than-empty, so the idea of having too much energy can seem confusing. But here's the thing about energy: We tend to assume we have only enough to do what we're trying to do. We don't raise our energy to meet the demands, we lower our energy to meet our expectations. But as you lean into a compelling vision, as you begin to manage your energy by changing how you relate to certain relationships or events or environments or you begin removing certain relationships or events or environments, you will begin to experience a strange feeling: you'll have more energy than you know what to do with.

So what do we do then?

As Andrew leaned into his energy, he discovered he had more to give than he could possibly use just on the ice. He had more to give both at home and at his Ladd Foundation, an organization he and his wife, Brandy, also a client of the firm (we love coaching families), formed to provide children access to resources that would help with their health and well-being through what he called the 1616 approach. The notion of 1616 (Andrew's number is 16) is the "buffalo mindset." It comes from the idea that when a storm hits, every animal turns and runs away to escape. But buffalo calmly band together and head into the storm together. Andrew's 1616 programs teach kids to adopt the buffalo mindset and to band together to face life's inevitable storms. Andrew took on the buffalo mindset himself. With the help of his team working on him—and the team he was working with—he banded together with them and found he had more energy than ever before.

Chris' story is similar. When the pandemic hit in 2020, fortunately all the coaches in our firm were able to keep our jobs and keep paying the bills. But Chris wanted to go beyond that. So he put out word that he was willing to do free coaching calls for anyone who was negatively impacted by the lockdowns and market shifts due to the pandemic. Hundreds of people responded. He spent an entire month doing almost nothing but coaching people all over the world, for free.

What do we do with extra energy? We give it away.

Interestingly, generosity isn't simply something we do with excess energy. It's also a fantastic way to *create* energy. This is another one of the paradoxes of life. Many people wait until they're full to be generous. But what we've learned is that you'll never be full until you start serving others.

ENERGY AND ITS RELATIONSHIP TO GROWTH, LOVE, OWNERSHIP, AND VISION

This is how the value of love intersects with energy and vision and growth. Vision is a picture of the future that creates passion in you for what could be and should be. Having a vision unlocks new energy. The more ownership and responsibility you take for your life, your vision, and the more responsibility you take for your energy, the more energy you'll have. Taking responsibility creates progress, and progress creates energy. Loving your life and vision creates energy and having more energy can be used to love. The more energy and love you have for your vision, the more you grow. The more you grow, the more energy you have to continue to grow. It just expands and expands.

All this energy created from love and ownership and vision

and growth has to be harnessed. Energy unrestrained is like a nuclear explosion. So what's the reactor that harnesses the energy and funnels it into productive activity?

Integrity.

 Want to go deeper on this topic? We've developed free resources for you and your team for each chapter, including discussion questions, recorded interviews with our coaches, and more. To access, scan the QR code or go to www.novus.global/book/chapter9.

CHAPTER 10

MAXIMIZING YOUR WORD

Being a person of integrity is a mountain with no top—you have to learn to love the climb.

→ WERNER ERHARD

Everyone Hates Chris—Jell-O Runs—The Holy Grail—Work It Harder, Make It Better—Hannibal Lecter: Man of His Word—Dimmer Knob, Not Light Switch—A Mother's Commitment—Mowin' in the Rain

I have a recurring nightmare in which I'm trying to catch up to someone. I'm pumping my legs as hard as I can, but I'm not really moving anywhere, and I'm disoriented and confused. I'm doing everything there is to be done mechanically in order to move quickly, but it's as if as soon as my feet hit the pavement, I can't get any traction. It feels like the ground gives way, like I'm running in Jell-O. In my dream, I'm simply moving too slow.

While this is just a dream, sometimes that's how it can feel while we're awake too. Sometimes it can feel as if there are goals or desires that we want that feel just out of reach. We know we're working hard. After all, that's what high performers do. But sometimes it feels like for all this hard work we should be moving, you know, *faster*.

While I still haven't figured out what to do with my dreams (therapy?), thankfully I've learned how to not feel that way when I'm awake. The principles in this chapter have helped create traction in my own life and helped teams that we've worked with move at speeds they never thought possible.

→ **"The world suffers from both evil people with integrity and good people with low integrity."**

In that way, it's a shame that this chapter had to be last. If you made it this far, I want you to know: this is one of the most powerful principles anyone can ever apply to their lives and often creates the most amount of forward movement with our clients. When our coaches do trainings with teams, they start by saying, "We're here to give you tools to help you get twice as much done as you currently do now." Some people get excited about this, but most people don't. Most people don't want to be twice as productive as they are now. Let's be real: that sounds kind of exhausting.

But then our coaches say, "What if we could help you get twice as much done in half as much time?" Now people's ears perk up. Who doesn't want more time? It was the whole "time" thing that was making us resistant to getting more done in the first place—after all, who has time to be twice as productive? And then we put the cherry on top when our coaches say, "We're here to help you get twice as much done, in half as much time *with increased satisfaction.*"

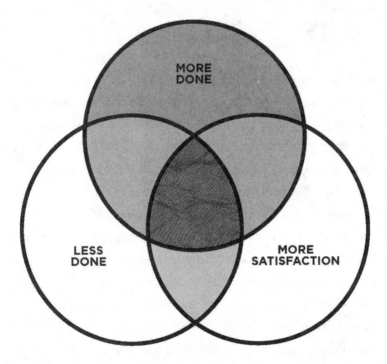

To us, that's the holy grail of meta performance. Anyone can be more productive. You just have to work more hours. Of course, this has massive limits—there are only twenty-four hours in the day—and massive costs if you burn yourself out. But to increase productivity in *less* time? Then maybe we could go on that vacation or start that hobby or spend more time with friends and family. Problem is, you can be more productive in less time and still be miserable. That's why we care about increasing your satisfaction. To do all three is to increase not just the quantity of what you produce but the quality of your life. That's meta performance.

Get More Done	In Less Time	With More Satisfaction	Bullseye
Get More Done	In More Time	With More Satisfaction	Too Busy
Get Less Done	In Less Time	With More Satisfaction	Less Productivity
Get Less Done	In Less Time	With Less Satisfaction	Not Satisfied

So if you want to get more done in less time with increased satisfaction, you might be surprised to read that the easiest way is to upgrade your integrity. When our coaches suggest this to people, they are usually met with resistance. Oftentimes people get offended, mainly because they have all sorts of different definitions of what *integrity* means. For most people, *integrity* means "morality." It means whether or not you're a good or decent person. But we at Novus Global define the word *integrity* the same way Harvard business professor Michael C. Jensen does. He is also the founder and chairperson of the Social Science Research Network and wrote the catchiest-titled paper ever: "Integrity: A Positive Model that Incorporates the Normative Phenomena of Morality, Ethics, and Legality." In an interview with *Rotman Management Magazine*, he explains there's a certain kind of integrity that is not a moral or ethical value. Rather, he says, "Integrity [as we're defining it] . . . has nothing to do with good versus bad." He's not talking about whether you're nice to your neighbor or don't kill anybody.

That's a fine definition of *integrity*, but in the coaching context, we're talking about something else. Jensen continues, "Think for a moment about the Law of Gravity: there is no such thing as 'good' or 'bad' gravity; like integrity [as we're defining it], it just 'is.'"[1]

INTEGRITY AND WORKABILITY

Another way to understand this unique perspective of *integrity* is in terms of "workability." A car has integrity when it *works*. If a car doesn't work, it's lacking some kind of integrity. Architects will often talk about a bridge or building having "structural integrity"—does it do what it is designed to do? Does it hold up under the weight of intended use? So when we look at our lives, or teams or systems, we can ask: does this system have integrity? Does this system *work*? Does my life work? Does this team work? Does it hold up under the weight of intended use? If it doesn't work, if it doesn't hold up, it's because it has some deficit in its integrity.

So what makes something "work"? Jensen offers this simple definition: things work when people do what they say they're going to do, when they say they're going to do it. We'll give a more nuanced definition later in this chapter, but this is where we'll start for now. With this definition, I sometimes joke that Hannibal Lecter from *Silence of the Lambs* had more integrity than most people. After all, he said he was going to eat you, and then he ate you. Using "integrity," in this case, is not a moral statement. Obviously, we can all agree you shouldn't eat people, but that's not what we're talking about. We're talking about a person's capacity to declare what they're going to do and then follow through with it. The truth of the matter is that many times evil people have more integrity than good people. Evil people make horrible plans and then execute them. Yet I know a lot of good people high on good intentions and low in integrity. They say they're going to serve the world in some important way and then never do. They say they're going to volunteer someday, and they never do. They say they're going to make things right with their estranged family member and never do. The world suffers from both evil people with high integrity and good people with low integrity (more on this in the final chapter).

But what does all this have to do with getting more done in less time with increased satisfaction?

WHEN TEAMS LACK INTEGRITY

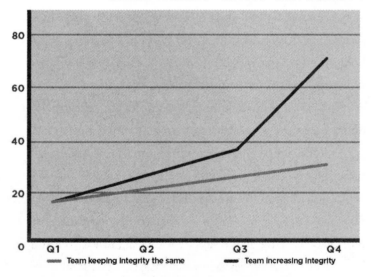

Ever notice how most things take longer to accomplish than you think? Why is this? Part of it is because we're pretty bad at guessing how long certain tasks or projects will take, but also because we often don't do the things we said we would do in the first place. We stall.

We avoid. We do all the things that aren't really necessary or vital to accomplishing our goals and instead fill our time with a lot of work that makes us feel productive without actually being productive (here's looking at you, email). Generally speaking, the more you do what you say you're going to do, the faster you get things done. And this is compounded on teams or when groups of people work together, because now it's not just about you doing what you said you'd do, but everyone else doing what they said they'd do when they said they'd do it. Most people understand what it's like to be on a team and try to complete a project together—usually there's some kind of time line for completion. The less integrity a group of people has together, meaning the less they do what they say they're going to do, the longer it takes to get something done. Conversely, the more integrity a group has, the shorter that time line gets.

WHAT SLOWS DOWN INTEGRITY— OR, RUNNING ON JELL-O

Quickly, how does it feel when you *don't* do what you say you're going to do? If you're human, you feel bad. Specifically, when we know there is something we ought to do or want to do, and we don't do it, we feel shame, even if it's just a little bit. And rather than doing something about it, we sometimes make other people feel like they're wrong, or it's their fault. We cast blame. We gossip. We play the victim. All this is a colossal waste of time. Every second we spend feeling bad about things is precious energy wasted.

Another common thing we do on teams is say we're going to do something, then don't do it, *and then hope no one notices*. We spend a lot of time hiding, hoping no one finds out. As Robert Keegan and Lisa Laskow Lahey write in their book, *An Everyone*

Culture, "Most people have two jobs at work. The first is the one they're paid to do. The second is covering their own ass." They note from their research that many people think they're "burnt out" from work, when what they're burnt out from is pretending, hiding, and feeling ashamed and experiencing a lack of progress in their jobs.

Here's another pop quiz: Do you think people are more productive or less productive when they're busy feeling ashamed and hiding? This answer isn't hard to guess. Even a little shame and hiding slows leaders down. It slows down our working relationships. It slows down our ability to produce. It slows down our ability to perform. When we're in meetings with people we've broken promises to, even small ones, we don't show up as our full selves.

High performers are oftentimes the grossest offenders when it comes to lack of integrity. As high performers, they think they don't have to be on time. "Hey, I'm a high performer. I don't have to get that email out. I'm busy!" Most companies let high performers off the hook. There's a kind of quid pro quo, under-the-table agreement with high performers and the company: you keep your numbers up, and we'll look the other way when you do things we don't let others get away with. Generally, the more important you appear to be to the company, the less important it is that you have integrity. We let CEOs arrive late to meetings and phone calls. "They're busy." We let the delayed response to an email go. "They must be too busy or have too important of a job to get back to us." Then what tends to happen in these organizations is everyone looks to this leader and copies that behavior. It becomes the norm, accepted, just another day at the office—where people arrive when they want, respond at their leisure, and join meetings "when they can." But here's the deal, decreasing integrity trickles down. If the CEO allows themselves to be sixty seconds late, their managers allow themselves to be six minutes late, and then the next leader down will let themselves be sixteen minutes late. This is why it can feel like a team is running on Jell-O, never getting where they want to go. Everyone is bogged down with excuses for why they are late or have stories for why something isn't done. It's an incredible time and energy drain, and everything starts to feel like it's moving in slow motion. Everyone on a team that lacks integrity feels exhausted, depleted, and shredded. Not because they're not going anywhere, but because they're running on a treadmill of *their own* delayed promises.

I often say one of the best forms of self-care is increasing the level of integrity you have. Because how does it feel when you say you're going to do something and then you do it? It feels amazing! How many of us love to cross items off our list of things to do? There's nothing better than putting your head on the pillow at night, knowing all the things you set out to do that day are *done*. I recall one night I went to go to bed, and I remembered an email I had committed to sending that

> → "One of the best forms of self-care is increasing the level of integrity you have."

day. I could have said, "I'll send it in the morning." Or I could have said, "They won't remember." I could have blamed my "long and busy day" or distractions. But I got out of bed, went up to my dark office, popped open my laptop, typed out the email, and pushed send. It felt great. I fell asleep easily that night, knowing I did what I said I was going to do. That's a fantastic form of self-care and a way to build self-efficacy.

WHERE WOULD YOU BE IF YOU HONORED YOUR COMMITMENTS?

Integrity moves our lives forward. When our coaches do trainings about integrity and making commitments, they ask the crowd, "How many of you have ever broken your resolutions?" Everyone raises her hand. Then they ask, "What would your life be like if you had kept them?" People say:

"I'd weigh less."

"I'd have better relationships."

"I'd have more money."

"I'd make more art."

"I'd make a bigger difference in the lives of others."

"I'd have more freedom."

All the things you want out of life are on the other side of keeping your word or honoring your word. Everything.

The body and health you want.

The relationships you want.

The career you want.

The money you want.

The lifestyle you want.

That seemingly impossible vision you want for yourself.

There's not a single dream, not a single vision, that you have that you'll be able to create without honoring your word and increasing the level of integrity in your life.

→ "There's not a single dream, not a single vision, that you have that you'll be able to to create without honoring your word and increasing the level of integrity in your life."

Because this is true, here are a few tips and ideas that will help you and your team or community begin to put more weight on the bar when it comes to increasing your own integrity.

1. LOOK AT INTEGRITY LIKE A VOLUME KNOB

When we're talking about integrity, it's important not to look at it as either "you have it or you don't." It's not a light switch that's either on or off. It's more like a volume knob. Everybody has integrity. Every day even the most horrible human beings make and keep dozens, if not hundreds, of commitments to themselves. They wake up on time. Or brush their teeth. We declare things are going to happen and then we make them happen all the time. So the question isn't do you have integrity or not. The question is: *How do you turn up the volume on your integrity in order to get more done in less time, with increased satisfaction?*

When a client decides to work with us, they sign a contract saying they're going to be on time to coaching calls. And it never fails, especially with high performers: eventually, they're running late. And it surprises them when they hop on, and they're sixty seconds late, and I say, "Hey, you're late."

Instantly, they reply, "Well . . . you know . . . like . . . it's only . . . been sixty seconds . . . because this person wanted to talk to me, and my last meeting went long."

It's amazing to me to see these high-powered, high-functioning people become victims of other people in their lives. Of course, if their daughter was kidnapped by terrorists or something, then it wouldn't be that big a deal. What people often don't understand is that honoring your word doesn't mean there is zero margin for error. Rather, honoring your word is acknowledging that you aren't always going to keep your word, but can be committed to being honest about when you break your word, owning the impact, and continually working to increase the level of integrity in your life.

2. GO FOR 100 PERCENT OF YOUR COMMITMENTS 100 PERCENT OF THE TIME

The commitments we tend to keep the least are the ones we make to ourselves. When we start to honor the commitments we make to ourselves, we increase our capacity for integrity. If you want to start becoming a high-integrity person, you need to start being honest with yourself about the commitments you keep. When you do this, you're going to create environments and relationships of high integrity everywhere you go.

When we go into companies to coach, one of the things we invite our clients to do is resolve to keep 100 percent of their commitments 100 percent of the time.

Most people balk. "No way. I am not doing that."

Then we say, "Okay. So then what percent of your commitments would you like for us to expect you to keep?"

Some say, "I want you to expect me to keep 90 percent of my commitments. That feels reasonable." Others will say, "I want you to expect me to keep 80 percent." We even have people say, "50 percent seems doable."

Then I say, "So if I ask you to do something, I can expect you to keep 80 percent of your commitments? Do you think I can trust that you're going to do that one thing?"

The answer is no. I don't know if this is the 80 percent when you usually do things or the 20 percent when you usually don't.

So I don't know what I am going to get. For all practical purposes, anything less than 100 percent amounts to 0 percent when it comes to trust. This is why we advocate for a 100 percent commitment 100 percent of the time.

This may seem unreasonable, but bear with me. The main reason we do this is because of the nature of the purpose of commitments. The primary purpose of commitments isn't what people think it is. Most people think that the sole purpose of making commitments is to keep them. But it's not. One purpose of commitments is to keep them. But another purpose of commitments is growth. We make commitments not simply so that we can keep them but so that we can become the kind of people who keep more and more significant types of commitments.

One example of this is wedding vows. When people make wedding vows, those vows are rarely "realistic." We usually say something to the effect that we'll always, which implies 100 percent of the time, cherish, protect, provide, love—richer, poorer, in sickness and health, etc. But are those vows realistic? If you're married right now, do you always *cherish* your spouse? If you've ever been short with them or rude or critical, even just in your own head, the answer is no. Married people violate parts of their vows regularly. So what should we do? Should we make the vows "more realistic"?

Pastor: Repeat your vows after me. "I promise ..."

Husband: I promise ...

Pastor: "To honor and cherish you ..."

Husband: To honor and cherish you ...

Pastor: "Eighty percent of the time ..."

Husband: Eighty percent of the time ...

Pastor: "And 50 percent of the time when your mother is in town."

No, we don't make vows like that, because the vows aren't meant to simply be something that we keep. The vows are actually more than that. They're not meant to be merely achievable. They're also meant to be aspirational. They're meant to be a North Star that we are constantly aiming for. They allow us to *grow* in our capacity to love another person, which is why in our work we will hold that as the primary goal of keeping commitments—to help us grow. Keeping our commitments increases our capacity to create. The goal isn't for you to always do what you say you're going to do, because that leads to making lesser commitments. The goal is to explore what we're capable of, and it's leveraging the power of commitments to do that.

3. STORE YOUR WORD OUTSIDE YOUR HEAD

Of course, most of us aren't even aware of the commitments we're making. We don't usually write down what we're committed to, so we're not aware of what commitments we're breaking. When you call someone on a broken commitment, they're usually surprised (or offended) that you remembered. Then they tend to manufacture a bunch of excuses. All this slows down productivity. Part of the journey of increasing your integrity is to be aware of the commitments you make. In order to grow in this, we ask, "Where do you store your word?"

Most people store their word in the gray matter between their ears. This is the worst possible place to keep your word. The world inside your mind is like a painting of an acid trip on a merry-go-round circling the sun. It is a horrible place to keep your word. We all forget things. Our memories are awful. Ever been at a busy meeting with loads of details? And you think you're going to remember it all? Forget about it. Literally. Our short-term memory can only hold about seven pieces of information at one time—for about twenty seconds. Scientists estimate that over the course of our lifetime the modern human brain will hold up to one quadrillion pieces of information. You have about seventy thousand thoughts per day. The chances of you forgetting what you're committing to is pretty high.[2]

The solution to this is writing down your commitments. We recommend that you take that to the next level and store your word outside your head in a digital space that is semipublic, meaning where at least one other person can see what you're up to. In our work with clients, and in all our meetings at the firm and institute, we use an online product called Asana. All our commitments are captured in Asana. Not only can I see it but other designated people can see it too. My assistant can see it. If I'm working with a client, both my client and I can see it. All this increases the probability I will keep my commitments. Digital isn't necessarily that important, but it does help because it makes it easier to share. You can also set up digital reminders.

If you want to add more weight to the integrity bar, try this: Some experts argue that the best place to store your word is your calendar. If it doesn't exist in your calendar, you're not committed to it. Since all commitments take time, and most high performers overcommit and then underdeliver, what does a powerful commitment look like? It looks like what Steve Hardison, one of the best coaches in the world, calls a "mother's commitment."

4. COMMIT LIKE A MOM

Most people understand there is a powerful bond between a mother and her child. If a child is in danger, starving, or hurting, you better watch out, because most mothers will do whatever they need to do in order to protect their child. There is a tenacity and ferocity to a mother's *commitment* to protecting her children. What Steve suggests is that everyone can tap into their version of this kind of commitment to the things they care about. Every human being, regardless of whether they are a mother or not, has the capacity to commit to things in their life in a way that mimics a mother's commitment to her child. This isn't necessarily meant to be literal, but imaginative. When we work with clients we ask, "What would it look like for you to commit to things as ferociously as a mother commits to protecting her child?" Imagine being so committed to something that no matter what gets in the way you still attack that goal like a lioness might attack a jackal who threatens her cubs, or protect your progress with the same passion that a mother protects her kids.

Of course, you don't have to access this gear all the time. But in coaching we invite people to explore what this would look like surgically to help you get to the next level of whatever your vision is.

5. UPGRADE YOUR DEFINITION OF *AUTHENTICITY*

If you want to upgrade your integrity, we want to invite you to upgrade your definition of another word: *authenticity*. The most common use of the word *authentic* is when we're doing the things that come most naturally to us. For example, we often dress in a way that expresses how we most naturally feel. We call this "authentic." Or when we speak and act in ways that feel most natural to us, we say we're being "authentic." The good news is, this is a perfectly wonderful use of the word *authentic*. And designing a life or teams around people doing what comes most naturally to them is an important aspect of leadership, both for yourself and others.

The bad news is, you can overdose on that kind of authenticity, especially when you're trying to learn something new. For example, there's nothing "authentic" for most people about learning a new language. It's time consuming, often expensive, awkward, and borderline psychologically traumatic to create a whole new linguistic schema in your mind other than your native language. When people learn a new language as adults so they can thrive in a new culture, it's really impressive. It's really beautiful. But it's not authentic. Not at first.

Or take going to the gym. Very few people enjoy going to a gym. They may enjoy *leaving* the gym after a great workout. But as they walk into a gym, most people are going against *what feels natural*. If people wait until exercise feels authentic before going to the gym, they will never go to the gym.

That's why in our work we don't define *authenticity* solely on your feelings. Feelings come and go. Feelings can change over time. We don't base authenticity only on your feelings, but on *what you're committed to*.

For example, I wake up every morning and exercise. Every morning. I go to my own gym in my building when I'm home, and I look for gyms when I'm on the road, and if one is unavailable I have a "safety net" series of exercises I can do from anywhere to maintain my routine. Honestly, it never feels natural. It may someday. But not today. Every morning I wake up, I don't *want* to work out. But I do it anyway. I do it not because it's authentic to how I feel but because it's authentic to who I'm committed to being. I'm committed to being the kind of guy who never misses a workout.

And so I work out every day.

That's authentic to me because I decided for it to be.

But I wasn't always this way. In fact, when I was younger, I was nothing like this.

BECOMING A PERSON OF YOUR WORD

Back when I was in college, my roommate Chris said to me, "Jason, one of my favorite things about you is that you're a dreamer."

I said, "Oh, that's great!" What an encouraging friend Chris is.

But then he added, "The thing is, though, you have all these dreams, but you never do anything about them."

Everybody hates Chris.

But he was right. I was the king of procrastination. I remember in high school my two jobs were to take out the trash every week and mow the lawn. I have vivid memories of hearing the garbage truck clunking down the street while I was still in bed. I'd explode from the sheets like a cartoon character and try—usually in my underwear—to get the trash to the curb before the truck passed. I grew up in the suburbs of Kansas City, and you'd see thunderstorms crawl toward you on the horizon. You'd think that'd motivate me to mow the lawn *before* it rained. Nope. I'd wait till the first few sprinkles fell and then mow my dad's lawn like I was running a relay race. In college, I wouldn't pull an all-nighter to finish the essay. All-nighters are so much work. No, I'd wake up at four in the morning to start writing the paper and turn it in by eight. I did this because it "worked" for me. I got out of college in three years. So I figured I must be doing something right.

Of course, the ultimate procrastination is not doing something at all. Like Chris said,

I was a dreamer. One time I met with the president of our college to pitch him on transforming our school into the preeminent developmental institution in the world. I was nineteen. To my surprise, he said, "Sure." I never followed up.

But people can grow. Fast-forward to me at age thirty-nine. I am in a meeting, and someone on our team turns to me and says, "I want you to know one of the things I most appreciate about being on a team with you."

"Oh, what's that?" I asked.

"I know that when you dream out loud, and you talk about all the things you want to do, that you're actually going to do them."

It felt really good to hear someone say that about me. I had worked really hard to become that kind of person, and it felt even better to know that for the most part it was true.

Years ago I said we're going to start a coaching company that was going to be global, and it is. I said, "We're going to work with the most famous people on earth," and we are. I said, "We're going to start producing award-winning podcasts," and we did. I said, "We're going to write a bestselling book," and you're reading it right now. In my personal life, I tell my nephews, my sister, and my parents that I'm going to take them on amazing trips, and I do. I tell myself I'm going to work out every day, and I do. I've committed to giving away more time and money than I ever thought I could when I was nineteen, and I have.

Chris pointed out that I had a lot of room to grow at nineteen. What's exciting is I *still* have a lot of room to grow. We all do. And in the meantime, it feels really good to keep commitments. It feels amazing to reach beyond what once felt natural or "authentic" and became who I am today. I want everyone to enjoy the thrill of committing to things even when you don't know how you're going to do them. I want you to experience the thrill of doing them, then saying, "I didn't know I could do that." Just like a mother—so fiercely committed to her child—was able to lift a car off her child at the beginning of this book.

The reality is, you are a very fluid concept right now.[3] At any given moment, you can choose to be a meta performer. So that means:

You can use *vision* to reshape how you see the present and the past.

You can *grow* beyond the limits of what you think you are capable of today by choosing to *own* all the ways you're holding yourself back.

You can take *love* into the workplace and fiercely advocate for yourself and others.

You can expand your *energy* to give to the things that matter most and funnel that energy into making bold commitments and keeping them by honoring your *integrity*.

You can choose to GO LIVE.

 Want to go deeper on this topic? We've developed free resources for you and your team for each chapter, including discussion questions, recorded interviews with our coaches, and more. To access, scan the QR code or go to www.novus.global/book/chapter10.

COACHING FOR A BETTER FUTURE

But the noble make noble plans and by noble deeds they stand.

→ **YESHAYAHU, SON OF AMOZ, CIRCA 740 BCE**

See Ya Later, Vader—Lessons from Robert the Bruce—The Coach on Your Shoulder—Wiring $100,000 to Nigerian Princes—The Day You Die—One Starfish Sucks—What the World Needs ometimes I imagine what it would be like to coach fictional characters from my favorite movies or TV shows. How would you coach the Black Panther or Mrs. Maisel or Rey Skywalker? It gets really interesting when you think about coaching the villains—the Joker. Thanos. Walter White. Norman Bates. I've thought a lot about how a typical high-performance coach would coach Darth Vader. Considering that a typical high-performance coach helps a person figure out what they want and then how to get it, the conversation with Darth Vader would go something like this:

Coach: Hey, Darth, what's your dream? What do you want to accomplish that you could only accomplish with a coach?

Darth: I want to blow up a planet and kill billions of people!

Coach: Way to dream big, buddy! [jotting some notes down] Okay, so that's the vision. So what's getting in the way?

Darth: [thinks about it for a second] Well, we've hired some pretty bad engineers. The Death Star has a *significant* security flaw. And also, my son wants to kill me.

Coach: Why does your son want to kill you?

Darth: I don't want to talk about it.

Coach: Okay, so those are two pretty big problems. Which one would you like to solve first: Security flaw or killer son?

Darth: Security flaw.

Coach: Right. Well, what could you do about the whole "security flaw" problem?

Darth: I could suffocate and kill the engineers by pinching the air with my fingers.

Coach: [looks up, surprised] How does pinching the air . . . never mind. Would killing the engineers actually solve the security problem?

Darth: [thinks about it] No. I guess not.

Coach: Well, then, what would?

Darth: I could hire some new engineers to fix the problem?

Coach: Good! That's one solution. I bet we can come up with a few more. You'll be fulfilling your dream of planetary genocide in no time!

Darth: Yay!

Obviously, this is ridiculous at best and horrifying at worst. Here's the point: we shouldn't want everyone's dreams to come true. While very few people are as simplistically evil as a movie villain, that doesn't mean we shouldn't evaluate the quality of our dreams and who they affect. Some people's dreams are other people's nightmares. Walt Disney may have famously said, "If you can dream it, you can do it," but maybe this isn't always a good thing. The ancients understood this. There's an old Italian saying: *Quando dio vuole castigarci, ci manda quello che desideriamo.*

This translates to "When the gods wish to punish us, they answer our prayers."[1]

James of Jerusalem put it this way in a letter nineteen hundred years earlier:

"We have because we do not ask. And when we ask, we ask with the wrong motives."[2]

We live in a world where we have more power and support than ever to make our dreams come true. Because of this, maybe we should be as concerned about the quality of our dreams as we are about the fulfillment of our dreams.

> → "Some people's dreams are other people's nightmares."

That's what this last chapter is about.

ABUSING GOOD THINGS

In his book *Factfullness*, author Hans Rosling invites us into a paradox: the world is full of suffering for everyone, *and* it's the best it's ever been for everyone on earth.

This is a hard paradox to grasp. I see some people championing a narrative that the world is going to hell in a handbasket, and anyone who celebrates progress is inherently against whatever suffering still remains. I see this mostly in my own country, the United States. If you say anything positive about America to some people I know, they attack you for succumbing to the "myth of American exceptionalism." But then I have other friends who seem to be allergic to any honesty about the growing challenges on America's horizons. They seem to ignore the plight of others, both today and historically. Both these groups are wrong. Not only are they wrong; they are foolishly wrong. But foolishness is rarely *totally* wrong. Foolishness is usually *partially* right.

In fact, I like to say that foolishness is wisdom, *misused*. Something I say often to our teams is that if you don't know how something can be misused you're probably misusing it. One quick example of this is empathy. Over the last fifteen years, I've witnessed an explosion of books, articles, conferences, and rhetoric around empathy. In many circles, it's become the de facto virtue, more important than all others. But this is wrong. While many situations could benefit from much more empathy, other situations could use much less of it. In his book *Against Empathy: The Case for Rational Compassion*, Harvard psychologist Paul Bloom shows how being too empathetic actually causes pain and suffering for others. It can lead us to pass bad policies that might make us feel better in the moment but will worsen everything down the road.

It can cause a parent to become an enabler of their drug-addicted teenager. Making empathy the chief of virtues strangely leads to more suffering in the world. My colleague Jean-Marie Jobs first introduced me to Edwin Friedman's term *empathy extortion*, in which people think they can demand you to feel a certain way toward them or else you're automatically wrong. Or when feelings of harm become more important than facts that could be helpful. You can actually sociologically overdose on empathy—the same way you can overdose on water. A good thing becomes a bad thing when it's used in incorrect proportions. The point is this: most people have never thought about how empathy can be damaging. And the less we think about that—or the more we are offended by it—the more in danger we are of weaponizing empathy.

And lest you think I'm being too hard on empathy, the same can be said for nearly anything. Anything can be weaponized, including the principles laid out in this book. Read that sentence again. It's easy to take the idea of growth and weaponize that into productivity porn, where it's "all growth, all the time," turning people into merely cogs in an unrelenting machine of more. It would be easy to take the idea of integrity and dogmatically punish people for missing a deadline or being late to a meeting. Or being so terrified of forgetting to do something or delaying a project that we sandbag our integrity and shrink our lives into what we know for sure we can handle. It would be easy to take the value of ownership and suck any empathy from it to where any time someone has been authentically attacked or hurt, you victim blame as an effort to protect the guilty.

That is why none of these values can take their place as the primary value in this conversation. No, none of these six values sit on the throne. Instead, these six values are what *the throne is made of*. That's what the essence of the multidox approach is about. As soon as you put one of these values on the throne, it becomes a tyrant that oppresses the other five. There is only one thing that deserves to be on any throne in any person's life. And too few make the quest to put it there.

BECOMING *HOMO SAPIENS*

In 1758 Carl Linnaeus, a Swedish biologist and physician, created Latin labels to explain the evolutionary history of humanity. Over 2 million years ago, there was *homo habilis* ("handy"), named so because of their first use of ancient tools. To our ancestors from 1.5 million years ago, Linnaeus gave the name *homo erectus* ("upright"), due to the progression of walking on all four limbs to walking on two legs. And then to our ancestors 300,000 years ago to today, he gave the phrase *homo sapien*. So if *habilis* means "handy," and *erectus* means "upright," then what does *sapien* mean?

It means "wisdom."

Linnaeus named us "wise."

If only naming made it so.

The story of human history is the story of humanity struggling to become wise. Thousands of years ago, long before King Solomon asked for wisdom to be a good king, each human being has been faced with the question, "What does it mean to be wise?" We've been asking that question since we were able to ask questions. This isn't a question about personal growth; it's a question about *moral* growth. What's unique about moral growth is how much slower it evolves than other types of growth, such as technological growth. As Martin Luther King Jr. once said, "Our military power has outrun our spiritual power. We have guided missiles and misguided men." It is easier to scale technology than it is to scale wisdom. It seems as though every generation has to relearn for itself what it means to be wise. As a general rule, you can't pass wisdom on to the next generation biologically. You can't breed wisdom. It's even difficult to pass on culturally, because it has to be chosen by the next generation of their own free will. And it seems that every generation rediscovers ancient wisdom forgotten by the previous generation and forgets wisdom previously understood by those who came before them.

Every generation is tempted to reject the wisdom passed on to it.

Furthermore, no one ever "arrives" at wisdom. You don't "become wise"—you can only grow in wisdom. Wisdom, it turns out, is a summitless peak. You can't overdose on wisdom. You can't get *too* wise. Wisdom, in the ancient world, was like happiness during the American Revolution. When America's founding fathers thought about "life, liberty, and the pursuit of happiness," they weren't thinking about faster cars or bigger houses or more zeros in your bank account. Happiness wasn't just about your right to do what makes you happy. Happiness was about your right to learn what's worth being happy about. Happiness, in the minds of women and men three hundred years ago, wasn't just about getting what you want. It was about learning to want what matters.

So what sits on the throne? Wisdom. Wisdom sits on the throne, inviting us to endlessly wrestle with how each of these values affects the others and how they should or shouldn't be applied in any specific context.

And it's not enough to just understand how they should be applied. If we want to be wise, we have to actually apply them. And when we do, we don't just become wise.

We become noble.

THE NOBLE PURSUIT

"Tell me, what does that mean to be noble? Your title gives you claim to the throne of our country, but men don't follow titles; they follow courage. Now, our people know you. Noble and common, they respect you. And if you would just lead them to freedom, they'd follow you. And so would I."

Randall Wallace wrote this speech for William Wallace, speaking to Robert the Bruce, for his 1995 film *Braveheart*. To me, the question he asks is *the* question: "What does it mean to be noble?".

Nobility is wisdom *applied*.

When we're talking about moving Beyond High Performance, we're talking about achieving both → **"Nobility is wisdom, applied."**

breadth and depth in life. And we're not just talking about increasing your net worth or square footage of your house and those types of things. We're talking about so much more. We're going *beyond* that.

The word *beyond* means "adding to something," or it can also mean "more important than." You can go beyond high performance by increasing your performance, but you could also go beyond high performance for something that is more important, more deep, more life-giving than performance itself.

To go beyond high performance and become a meta performer is to fiercely care both about the quality of your life and the qualit of your impact. It's about creating a noble future. A noble future is one in which we grow in our capacity to care about the quality of everyone else's life, not merely our own. It's where going beyond high performance means not just achieving more but being a better person while doing so—and creating a better world and future. It requires a sense of morality and decency.

In order to truly be a meta performer, you need the courage to be *good*. Too many take a Hippocratic oath approach to goodness. The Hippocratic oath says, "Do no harm." So people think, *So long as I'm not hurting anybody, then that's good*. Even Google has its famous slogan: "Don't be evil." But the problem with this is treating "good" as the absence of something. "If I'm not evil, then I must be good." But good isn't the absence of evil. It's the opposite of evil. It's not enough to not do harm. *You have to create good*. A deep and fulfilling and rewarding life isn't found in "not doing evil." A deep and fulfilling and rewarding life is found in pursuing good. And that's good news, because we have way more potential to do good than any of us realize.

We just have to cultivate the imagination and communities and courage to unleash it. We have to upgrade our small definitions for *human goodness*.

BEYOND ONE STARFISH

Here's one example: many of you have heard the clichéd "starfish story." A guy is walking along the beach, and it's covered in starfish. He throws one back in. Another guy walks by and says, "Why did you do that? There's no point. There's too many. It makes no difference." And the guy who threw the starfish back in the ocean says, "It made a difference to that one."

Bear with me, but I actually hate that story.

Illustration by Micah Brenner

That's not a meta-performance story. If that guy really cared about starfish, he would have said to the person judging him, "Hey, why don't you help me? Why don't we call all our friends and family and get them out here, and we can get them all back in the water?" He would have asked himself the question, "How many starfish am I capable of helping?" The truth is, more than one. Almost everyone can do more than one. One is the minimum. If you're reading this, one for you is probably phoning it in.

Imagine if he left that day, did some research on current weather patterns, the warming of the ocean, and figured out a way to save the entire starfish population? What if in the process he brought awareness to the growing problem of pollution and dumping of plastics in our ocean, started a foundation, and then in the meantime founded a company that cleans out plastic bottles and makes those bottles into tents and medical supplies that helped people in war-torn countries? Maybe he wins a Nobel Peace Prize and makes groundbreaking discoveries in the worlds of oceanography, biology, ecology, and business. And what if his family got involved, and they got to do all this together, like a giant science project. What if his cause also improved his relationships with his wife, his children, and the people he loved while doing so? What if with all the money he made from all his accomplishments he was able to pour it into his other passion projects, and those of his friends, who were also doing incredible things? What if he didn't stop at one starfish?

I'm not suggesting that every person should win the Nobel Peace Prize, save the ocean, and build a multibillion-dollar industry with their perfect families by their side. Nor am I saying not to help someone in need if it's only one person.

I am saying that every person should ask themselves:

What's the most I can do? And how can I explore what I'm capable of in those things that matter most?

As we wrap up our time together, I hope you become obsessed with that question. Sure, I hope you get other things, like that you use this book to create, say, more wealth. But more than that, I hope you read this book and choose to become the kind of person who uses wealth to serve the world. There are two prayers I often pray when I talk to God. One is: "God, make me wealthy." This is fine. But the second prayer is more important, which is, "God, make me the kind of person who you can trust with wealth."

Illustration by Micah Brenner

If I had to pick between the two, I'd pick the second one. But I'd like to have both, and I think most people think they have to pick one over the other or pick one at the expense of the other.

THE MOST IMPORTANT THING TO BE FIRST AT

In the middle of the pandemic, a journalist from *Forbes* reached out to me and asked, "What are you seeing business leaders do in response to COVID-19?"

And I said, "I can't tell you what I see business leaders doing, but I can tell you what we're doing. We have a maxim in our firm, which is: 'Those who serve today will lead tomorrow.'"

Those who serve today will lead tomorrow.

During the pandemic, we reached out to our networks, and we just started coaching as many people as we could for free. Our coaches donated hundreds of hours to people around the world. Of course, we ended up working with some amazing companies and individuals, who eventually hired us to work with them. We served, and now we are leading. But we didn't serve as a business development strategy. It wasn't a bait and switch. We didn't serve to sell. We served to serve.

My hope and prayer for all who are reading this book is that you become obsessed. I hope you become as obsessed with maximizing your character as you would with maximizing your power. Meta performers are obsessed with both. That's what it truly means to go beyond high performance.

The parent company of the Meta Performance Institute and Novus Global is called the Noble Company. The Noble Company exists to invest in leaders and companies who are excited about noble pursuits—not just becoming better, wealthier, or more successful, but to become a steward of their lives for the benefit of all. .

But how do we do this?

METABOLIZE, DON'T JUST SYNTHESIZE

Up until the Industrial Revolution, information was power. Very few people could read. Fewer people had books. Those who had access to information ruled. During the information revolution, all that changed. Suddenly, anyone, anywhere could Google anything; therefore "knowing something" became largely, though not entirely, democratized. It was no longer enough to "know something"—knowing had given way to *synthesizing*. Today those who can take in all the information and synthesize it (metadata analytics) hold the power. Hedge funds and megacorporations hire scores of bright young analysts and programmers and build supercomputers to collect and analyze massive amounts of data. But even in the upcoming synthetic age, it won't be enough to know, it won't be enough to synthesize. The leaders of tomorrow will be the ones who are experts at 1) *metabolizing* information and 2) creating cultures of metabolization. To metabolize something isn't just to understand it but for it to sink so deep into your being that it shapes and animates every moment of your life. Just like when you eat food, and it metabolizes and animates your daily life, we must do the same thing with wisdom. This is what great leaders do. Great leaders help you metabolize information and convert it into energy in your life. They build environments oriented toward metabolization. And I believe the most powerful environments for metabolization are relationships. For as long as human consciousness has existed, we have intentionally designed relationships to help people metabolize powerful information. Families. Mentors. Coaches. Gurus. Religions. Schools. They are all relational environments designed for you to metabolize information into your life. It has always been this way and probably always will be. So I want to ask you:

What kind of relationships are you building to help you metabolize the most powerful information in the world?

These kinds of relationships are becoming increasingly rare. You don't drift into metabolizing relationships. You have to design them.

And one of the best ways to create that kind of relationship is to hire a coach.

I've had several clients of mine say, "I've got a little Jason on my shoulder now." When I first heard this, I got uncomfortable—after all, depending on little Jason's mood, I wouldn't necessarily want a little *me* on my shoulder. But over time I learned what they meant: they are slowly metabolizing our conversations into their lives. You see, coaching starts as an "external" relationship. Two separate people having a conversation. But just as the old cliché goes, "You are what you eat," the same goes for coaching: "You are what you coach into yourself." Over time, you will begin metabolizing what your coach challenges you to think and do in such a way that the voice no longer sounds like a coach's voice but yours. And once that happens, that's transformation.

Transformation is when you're not even aware that you reflectively and subconsciously operate with a new set of questions that produce new outcomes in your relationships, your finances, or whatever you are pursuing in life. Then that shifts into your teams, and then your community and organizations. Even your family will start habitually asking a different set of questions and seeing the world in new ways.

And now, one last story. This time about me working with a coach myself.

WORKING WITH THE ULTIMATE COACH

It's a unique experience wiring someone you've never met $100,000. No, this wasn't a "Nigerian prince" promising me millions if I could only give him my bank information to help him get out of his country. This was Steve Hardison, one of the world's best coaches. I wired him $100,000 so I could start working with him before we ever laid eyes on each other or shook hands. That may sound crazy to someone who has never personally hired a coach, but I'm a firm believer in doing myself what I'm asking my clients to do, and I believe in getting my skin in the game when it comes to coaching. Of course I could have bought a house, a sports car, or invested in crypto, but I chose to hire a coach.

Most people think hiring a coach is like going to get a haircut. Say it costs $50 for a haircut that takes an hour to get, so then you think, *That hairstylist makes $50 an hour.* With a coach, I would fly to meet with Steve twice a month for over a year. We met for two hours per session. I could break that time down and divide that by $100,000 and think, *That's the value I'm getting.* But that's not how coaching works. I paid that money not because I would get information for a day, a week, a month, or a year but because I would be using what Steve and I created together in those sessions for the rest of my life. I promise you: I'll be one hundred years old, and in the last week of my life I'll absolutely have some thought or action or choice that will have been directly influenced by Steve. You see, I didn't pay that $100,000 to work with Steve for just *a year*. I hired Steve so I could have his "coach on my shoulder" for the *rest of my life*. This morning I did my daily ritual of working out and grounding myself in who I was committed to be today. I learned that from Steve. Every single day of my life I am metabolizing and converting his thoughts into energy and benefitting from our relationship, even though we're not currently working together. That's the power of relationship. That's the power of coaching—when the lessons metabolize, they go with you for the rest of your life.

Now that may sound a little crazy. There's no way that a coach will remain with you for the rest of your life. But we do this with people in our lives all the time. If you have children, you know. As soon as your child is born, you carry them in your heart and mind everywhere you go. If you've ever been in love, you know that even when you're not with them, they are still with you. The love you have for them reshapes how you see circumstances, affects the choices you make, and even changes who you are. The same goes for great coaching and those who we allow to invest in us.

One of the most impactful things Steve did with me—and it has still stuck with me to this day—was during our last session he took me to his grave. Yes, you read that correctly. My coach has a tombstone, and on it is his name and a date in the future, marking his death. For as long as I live, I will never forget sitting beside the man whose grave we were visiting. He told me that for one of his birthdays his family planned his funeral. They came with a coffin, put him in it, drove to a funeral home, and he listened to others speak about him, his life, and legacy. One might argue that this is a bit morbid and bleak. But it's no different than the stoic philosophy of *memento mori* ("remember your death"). We will all die someday. We have a finite amount of time in this life, and if you do not stop to contemplate the ephemeral nature of your being, then you will waste your life—put off that which you could be doing, loving, growing, becoming.

When you live knowing that the clock is ticking, you act differently. Your life is not like information: it's a finite resource. There is only so much of it. And what will you do with it? Will you go on more dates with your wife? Take your kids out into the yard to play catch? Turn off the television and pick up a hobby? Volunteer or explore your generosity in some way? Call a loved one and tell them "thank you" or "I forgive you" or "I was stupid, and I'm sorry?"

Would you give more time and money to making the world a better place?

THE JOY OF META PERFORMANCE

The book you are holding is not something to memorize; it is something to metabolize. It wasn't a "how-to" but a "let's go." It was the workout, the energy drink, the bench press—it was the activity and the fuel you need to keep your body, mind, and soul agile, fit, and energized to go beyond high performance. And just like all eating and exercise, you never outgrow it. It never stops. You get to do it every day. And that, my friends, is the joy of meta performance. It is the process of becoming, of climbing the summitless peak. It's something you always are going to be doing and applying.

The parent company of the Meta Performance Institute and Novus Global is called the Noble Company. The Noble Company exists to invest in leaders and companies who are excited about noble pursuits not just becoming better, wealthier, or more successful but to become a steward of their lives for the benefit of all. This is because the world needs you to have a noble vision of a better future for everyone, not just your preferred tribe or group or company. The world needs you to know the difference between contentment and complacency and to dedicate your life to growing in the things that matter most. The world needs you to take radical ownership of your life and community—to be willing to wean yourself off the addiction we all have of blaming other people for our problems. The world needs you growing in your capacity to fiercely advocate, not simply for yourself, but for the good of others. The world needs you to learn the art of managing your own energy and putting that energy into serving others. The world needs you to do what you say you'll do and be who you say you are.

> → "The book you are holding is not something to memorize; it is something to metabolize. It wasn't a 'how-to' but a 'let's go.'"

The world needs you exploring how much nobility you are capable of creating with your one and only life.

The world needs you to GO LIVE.

The world needs you to go beyond high performance so you may look back at your life, many years from now, and see the countless people you got to love and serve and lead, and whisper with awe and gratitude:

"I didn't know I could do that."

Want to go deeper on this topic? We've developed free resources for you and your team for each chapter, including discussion questions, recorded interviews with our coaches, and more. To access, scan the QR code or go to www.novus.global/book/conclusion.

ACKNOWLEDGMENTS

I am grateful for so many who have helped make this book what it is.

First, I am grateful to God for everything in my life. I believe God gives us gifts to steward and use to make the world a better place. I hope this book does just that, and I am grateful for the opportunity to serve.

Beyond High Performance is in many ways all about leadership, and much of what I've learned about leadership I've learned from people who do their best to model their lives after the teachings of Jesus. A special thanks to four of them—Darren and Kari Wade, Reggie Epps, and Erwin McManus—for being spiritual leaders in my life and helping me fall in love with a spiritually vibrant community and to see that leadership is a spiritual endeavor.

I am one of the most fortunate people on earth to be surrounded by friends and family and colleagues and associates who partner with me to make art that I—and hopefully we—can be proud of. I'd like to thank the top coaches in the firm and faculty of the institute who I get to learn from and be challenged and inspired by on a regular basis: Dan Leffelaar, Amanda Jaggard, Jon Roberts, Janet Breitenbach, David Gerber, and Chris North. You all bring so much to my life. I love serving the world alongside you. Here's to all your noble dreams coming true.

I'm also incredibly grateful to the executives who lead to make all the magic of Novus Global and the Meta Performance Institute happen: Tricia Harding and David Miller and Joseph Thompson. You're astounding coaches in your own right, and yet you choose to give most of your time to leading coaches, which is like herding cats who are also on fire. You do the impossible on impossible budgets and time lines. Thanks for modeling the principles of this book so well.

I'd like to thank all the coaches in the firm and faculty at the institute who got their fingerprints on this book to help make it better and invite me to remove jokes that weren't funny: Kristin Frade, Rosanna Tomiuk, Melissa Caddell, Deb Foy, Laura Groen, Seth Schmidt, Lee Tracie-Stockburger, Laura Leffelaar, Lori Krueger, and Joseph King Barkley.

A huge shout-out to some of our clients who we talk about by name in this book. It's a vulnerable thing to admit you have a coach; it's a whole other thing to let a coach write about you by name to a large audience. Jeff Lambert, Daniel Moore, Andrew Ladd, Stephen Jeffs, and Bill Foy—I admire you all for doing the work to be at your best for those you love and a world that needs us all at our best.

And then, of course, there's the team who helped on the front lines of this book. Shannon Curran, you have been a rock star as you tried to hold together all the growing and shifting parts of my life while also wrangling the complexities of this book to the ground. I don't know how you did it, but I'm grateful you did. Mary Curran-Hackett, you were an absolute thrill to work with. Thank you for helping me get from zero to one and a whole lot farther. I'd hire you to write a book with me any day. Amanda Ayers Barnett and Rick Wolff, thank you for the wisdom you poured into this process. Steve, thanks for our incredible cover. Catri Dixon, you bring crazy ideas to life in a visual way that I just absolutely love. Colin Harman, thanks for making everything you touch better. Micah Brenner, thank you for making comic strips of silliness look profound. Keith Robinson and CJ Martindale, thanks for pushing this thing across the finish line and helping the trains run on time.

And to Myles Schrag and the team at Amplify Publishing Group, thanks for helping us get this message out into the world.

Finally, I'd like to thank my mom and dad: Sandy and Craig Jaggard. They raised two of the top coaches in this firm and both of the cofounders of the institute. Thank you for your unwavering support in everything I've ever attempted in my life. I'm proud to be part of your legacy of investing in others. I love you.

ENDNOTES

PREFACE

1 https://entertainment.howstuffworks.com/arts/circus-arts/
adrenaline-strength.htm

2 https://en.wikipedia.org/wiki/Hysterical_strength

INTRODUCTION

1 You can email me at jason@novus.global.

2 Seneca, *The Stoic Philosophy of Seneca: Essays and Letters.*

3 www.novus.global

4 www.mp.institute

5 https://www.amazon.com/
Maybe-You-Should-Talk-Someone/dp/1328662055

CHAPTER 1

1 Ericsson, K. A., Krampe, R.Th. and Tesch-Romer, C. (1993).
"The Role of Deliberate Practice in the Acquisition of Expert
Performance,"*Psychological Review*, 100, 393–394.

2   https://www.6seconds.org/2022/06/20/10000-hour-rule/

3   Michael Sullivan, "The Great Practice Myth:
Debunking the 10,000 Hour Rule," Six Seconds,
https://www.6seconds.org/2020/01/25/.
the-great-practice-myth-debunking-the-10000-hour-rule/.

4   https://workplaceinsight.net/half-of-people-have-quit-job-due-to-poor-work-relationship-with-boss/

CHAPTER 2

1   David Hoffeld, "Want To Know What Your Brain Does
When It Hears A Question?," Fast Company, February
21, 2017, https://www.fastcompany.com/3068341/
want-to-know-what-your-brain-does-when-it-hears-a-question.

2   Vicki G. Morwitz, Eric Johnson and David Schmittlein, "Does
Measuring Intent Change Behavior?," *Journal of Consumer
Research* 20, no. 1 (June 1993): 46–61.

3   Anthony G. Greenwald, Catherine G. Carnot, Rebecca Beach,
and Barbara Young, "Increasing Voting Behavior by Asking
People if They Expect to Vote," *Journal of Applied Psychology* 72,
no. 2 (1987): 315–318.

4   https://www.startrek.com/news/
how-lucille-ball-helped-star-trek-become-a-cultural-icon

CHAPTER 3

1   You can watch the entire thing here: https://vimeo.
com/26742776.

2   https://en.wikipedia.org/wiki/Greenlights_(book)

3   Frank Pallotta, "Pixar Movies Thanks to Napkin Sketches at a

Lunch Meetings," *Business Insider*, April 29, 2014, https://www.
businessinsider.com/pixar-movies-thanks-to-napkin-sketches-at-
lunch-meeting-2014-4.

CHAPTER 4

1   David Robson, "The 3.5% Percent Rule: How a Small Minority
    Can Change the World," BBC, May 13, 2019, https://www.bbc.
    com/future/article/20190513-it-only-takes-35-of-people-to-
    change-the-world.

2   https://www.abebooks.com/products/
    isbn/9781861053350?cm_sp=bdp-_-ISBN10-_-PLP

3   F. Scott Fitzgerald, "The Crack-Up: A Desolately Frank
    Document from One for Whom the Salt of Life Has Lost Its
    Meaning," *Esquire*, February 1936, https://classic.esquire.com/
    article/1982/2/1/the-crack-up.

4   Nassim Nicholas Taleb, *Skin in the Game* (New York: Allen
    Lane, 2018).

CHAPTER 5

1   "Understanding Unconscious Bias," NPR, July 15,
    2020, https://www.npr.org/2020/07/14/891140598/
    understanding-unconscious-bias.

2   Barry Schwartz, *The Paradox of Choice: Why More Is Less* (New
    York: HarperCollins, 2016).

3   Steve Zaffron and Dave Logan, *The Three Laws of Performance:
    Rewriting the Future of Your Organization and Your Life* (New
    York: Wiley, 2011).

4   "Urban Myth," In-N-Out Burgers, https://www.in-n-out.com/

menu/not-so-secret-menu.

CHAPTER 6

1   Maravich holds nearly every major NCAA scoring record, including most career points (3,667), highest career scoring average (44.2 ppg), most field goals made (1,387) and attempted (3,166), and most career 50-point games (28). And this was all before the invention of the 3-point line or the shot clock.

2   "Basketball is a way of life—The Pistol," YouTube, uploaded June 11, 2009, https://www.youtube.com/watch?v=gRp7a9NSzAQ.

3   Jeff Bezos and Walter Isaacson, *Invent and Wander: The Collected Writings of Jeff Bezos* (Boston: Harvard Business Press, 2020).

4   "Leadership Principles," Amazon, https://www.amazon.jobs/en/principles.

5   https://www.amazon.com/Being-Wrong-Adventures-Margin-Error/dp/0061176052

6   Christine Gross-Loh, "How Praise Became a Consolation Prize," *The Atlantic*, https://www.theatlantic.com/education/archive/2016/12/how-praise-became-a-consolation-prize/510845/.

7   Pretty good for a person who isn't good.

8   Ray Dalio, *Principles: Life and Work* (New York: Simon & Schuster, 2017).

CHAPTER 7

1   You can actually buy these online. Google "tablet dying plaque."

2   "Thinking, Fast and Slow | Daniel Kahneman | Talks at Google,"

YouTube, uploaded November 10, 2011, https://www.youtube. com/watch?v=CjVQJdIrDJ0.

3   Bill Foy, personal communication, July 15, 2022.

4   Ethan Kross, *Chatter: The Voice in Our Head, Why It Matters, and How to Harness It* (New York: Crown, 2021), 11.

5   "Miles Davis according to Herbie Hancock," YouTube, uploaded March 8, 2014, https://www.youtube.com/ watch?v=FL4LxrN-iyw.

CHAPTER 8

1   No offense to drunken sailors. I'm sure you're all sweet as pecan pie.

CHAPTER 9

1   Lois Kalchman, "Making NHL a Very Long Shot," Hockey Canada, January 25, 2003, https://www.hockeycanada.ca/en-ca/ news/2003-gn-001-en.

2   https://podcasts.apple.com/us/podcast/coach-ing-impact-on-all-facets-of-life-being-a/ id1570351111?i=1000526375797

3   Justin Sherman, "LeBron James' Contract Will See Him Get Paid $162 Per Second," *MARCA Baloncesto*, June 9, 2018, https:// www.marca.com/en/more-sports/2018/09/06/5b91622ae5fde-a344e8b4586.html.

4   www.novus.global/assessment

CHAPTER 10

1   Karen Christensen, "Integrity Is a Matter of a Person's

Word—Nothing More and Nothing Less," *Rotman Management Magazine* (Fall 2009): 16–20.

2   Shelby Burr, "10 Unforgettable Statistics About the Human Memory," *Artifact*, https://southtree.com/blogs/artifact/10-unforgettable-statistics-about-human-memory.

3   I stole this line from the movie *Hitch*.

CONCLUSION

1   This is actually a quote from Oscar Wilde in 1895 from his play *An Ideal Husband*. But I learned it (incorrectly) from an episode of *The West Wing* titled "The Two Bartlets."

2   James 4:3 NIV.

NOVUS ◯ GLOBAL

▶ Take Our Free Motivation Assessment

Discover how to maximize motivation in your life with our free 5i Assessment! This 20-minute assessment will let you know what your current top five "motivation makeup" is along with a personalized PDF explaining how to live a fully motivated life.

novus.global/5i

▶ Subscribe to The Beyond High Performance Podcast

Get weekly inspiration and leadership development with our three award-winning podcast shows all at the Beyond High Performance podcast channel. Our channel features interviews with top performers in the fields of business, government, sports and entertainment, along with behind-the-scenes round-table conversations with the coaches who work with the best to get better.

BEYOND
HIGH PERFORMANCE
P O D C A S T

novus.global/listen

▶ Join the Beyond High Performance Network

We have a network of leaders from around the world who are passionate about going beyond high performance. Joining the network gets you advance access to Novus Global's latest content and tools for leaders and coaches, webinars, and interviews with our top coaches and clients, private Q&A access to our best leaders, giveaways, and more!

BEYOND
HIGH PERFORMANCE
N E T W O R K

novus.global/network

▶ Bring a Novus Global Coach to Speak at Your Event

Want to maximize the impact of your live event? Bring in a coach from Novus Global or a faculty member from the Meta Performance Institute to give an inspiring keynote or in-depth workshop. We have world class communicators from diverse backgrounds speaking about how the principles from this book and our work can help your team, company or community go beyond high performance.

novus.global/speaking

ABOUT THE AUTHOR

JASON JAGGARD is an entrepreneur, producer, coach, and author whose work has been translated into over fifty languages and featured in *Fast Company*, *Forbes*, and *Entrepreneur* magazines. Jason is the founder of Novus Global, an executive coaching firm working with leaders of Fortune 100 companies, professional athletes, elected officials, and some of the most famous entertainers on earth. He is also a cofounder of the Meta Performance™ Institute, which helps people create six- and seven-figure incomes by learning how to powerfully coach high-performing leaders. He is the executive producer and co-host of the award-winning podcast *Beyond High Performance*, featuring interviews from coaches and people at the top of their fields exploring the question, "What am I capable of?"